The
SONS *of* MOSIAH

The

SONS *of* MOSIAH

Mark E. Petersen

Deseret Book

Salt Lake City, Utah

Note: The author wishes to make clear that this is not an official publication of The Church of Jesus Christ of Latter-day Saints. The opinions and views expressed are the author's, for which he alone is responsible.

Deseret Book Company
Salt Lake City, Utah

©1984 Deseret Book Company
All rights reserved
Printed in the United States of America
ISBN 0-87747-297-1
Library of Congress Catalog Card No. 83-73652

First printing February 1984

CONTENTS

Chapter 1

ENEMIES WITHIN AND WITHOUT

Rebellion within and persecution from without: this deadly combination faced the church in Zarahemla during the reign of King Mosiah. The trouble within arose where it was least expected, from the king's own home and the family of Alma, the presiding high priest.

Under the rule of Mosiah's father, the great king Benjamin, all the people had pledged solemnly to serve the Lord. But the little children did not understand this covenant and were not converted to it. Many in this rising generation rejected the faith as they grew up.

Chief among them were young Alma, son of the prophet Alma, and the four sons of Mosiah. They not only refused to follow their parents' teachings and turned to riotous living, but they also went among the Saints defying their own fathers and destroying the faith of those who would listen to them.

The scripture describes them in this way:

"Now the sons of Mosiah were numbered among the unbelievers; and also one of the sons of Alma was numbered among them, he being called Alma, after his father; nevertheless, he became a very wicked and an idolatrous man. And he was a man of many words, and did speak much flattery to the people; therefore he led many of the people to do after the manner of his iniquities."

He and the sons of Mosiah "became a great hinderment to the prosperity of the church of God; stealing away the hearts of the people; causing much dissension among the people; giving a chance for the enemy of God to exercise his power over them." (Mosiah 27:8-9.)

The record further describes the young men as "the vilest of sinners." (Mosiah 28:4.) It explains :

"There were many of the rising generation that could not understand the words of king Benjamin, being little children at the time he spake unto his people; and they did not believe the tradition of their fathers.

"They did not believe what had been said concerning the resurrection of the dead, neither did they believe concerning the coming of Christ.

"And now because of their unbelief they could not understand the word of God; and their hearts were hardened.

"And they would not be baptized; neither would they join the church. And they were a separate people as to their faith, and remained so ever after, even in their carnal and sinful state; for they would not call upon the Lord their God."

These unbelievers were "not half so numerous as the people of God; but because of the dissensions among the brethren they became more numerous.

"For it came to pass that they did deceive many with their flattering words, who were in the church, and did cause them to commit many sins." (Mosiah 26:1-6.)

Some members joined the dissenters in threatening the safety of the church.

The prophet Alma went to the king for advice, but as it was a religious, not a political matter, the king refused to take action. Alma then approached the Lord for direction. The Lord, by revelation, told him:

"Therefore I say unto you, Go; and whosoever transgresseth against me, him shall ye judge according to the sins which he has committed; and if he confess his sins before thee and me, and repenteth in the sincerity of his heart, him shall ye forgive, and I will forgive him also.

"Yea, and as often as my people repent will I forgive them their trespasses against me.

"And ye shall also forgive one another your trespasses; for

verily I say unto you, he that forgiveth not his neighbor's trespasses when he says that he repents, the same hath brought himself under condemnation.

"Now I say unto you, Go; and whosoever will not repent of his sins the same shall not be numbered among my people; and this shall be observed from this time forward." (Mosiah 26:29-32.)

Persecution immediately intensified.

"And now it came to pass that the persecutions which were inflicted on the church by the unbelievers became so great that the church began to murmur, and complain to their leaders concerning the matter; and they did complain to Alma. And Alma laid the case before their king, Mosiah. And Mosiah consulted with his priests.

"And it came to pass that king Mosiah sent a proclamation throughout the land round about that there should not any unbeliever persecute any of those who belonged to the church of God.

"And there was a strict command throughout all the churches that there should be no persecutions among them, that there should be an equality among all men." (Mosiah 27:1-3.)

In the midst of this bitter dissension stood Mosiah's own four sons and young Alma, destroying faith on all sides. They went about secretly, apparently in fear of the discipline of their fathers, leading people astray "contrary to the commandments of God, or even the king." (Mosiah 27:10.)

If the prophet Alma and king Mosiah could do nothing to control their own sons, the Lord could, because he had a work for them to do.

As the five were going about "rebelling against God, behold, the angel of the Lord appeared unto them; and he descended as it were in a cloud; and he spake as it were with a voice of thunder, which caused the earth to shake upon which they stood;

"And so great was their astonishment, that they fell to the

earth, and understood not the words which he spake unto them.

"Nevertheless he cried again, saying: Alma, arise and stand forth, for why persecutest thou the church of God? For the Lord hath said: This is my church, and I will establish it; and nothing shall overthrow it, save it is the transgression of my people.

"And again, the angel said: Behold, the Lord hath heard the prayers of his people, and also the prayers of his servant, Alma, who is thy father; for he has prayed with much faith concerning thee that thou mightest be brought to the knowledge of the truth; therefore, for this purpose have I come to convince thee of the power and authority of God, that the prayers of his servants might be answered according to their faith.

"And now behold, can ye dispute the power of God? For behold, doth not my voice shake the earth? And can ye not also behold me before you? And I am sent from God.

"Now I say unto thee: Go, and remember the captivity of thy fathers in the land of Helam, and in the land of Nephi; and remember how great things he has done for them; for they were in bondage, and he has delivered them. And now I say unto thee, Alma, go thy way, and seek to destroy the church no more, that their prayers may be answered, and this even if thou wilt of thyself be cast off.

"And now it came to pass that these were the last words which the angel spake unto Alma, and he departed."

All five young men fell to the earth, "for great was their astonishment; for with their own eyes they had beheld an angel of the Lord; and his voice was as thunder, which shook the earth; and they knew that there was nothing save the power of God that could shake the earth and cause it to tremble as though it would part asunder.

"And now the astonishment of Alma was so great that he became dumb, that he could not open his mouth; yea, and he became weak, even that he could not move his hands; therefore he was taken by those that were with him, and carried helpless, even until he was laid before his father.

"And they rehearsed unto his father all that had happened unto them; and his father rejoiced, for he knew that it was the power of God." (Mosiah 27:11-20.)

The prophet Alma called the members of the church together to see what God had done for his wicked son. They then joined his father in fasting and prayer for his recovery.

Chapter 2

ALMA IS BORN OF THE SPIRIT

Young Alma was unconscious for two days and nights as the Saints fasted and prayed for him. Then came the answer to their prayers. The Lord restored him to consciousness and renewed his strength.

Alma "stood up and began to speak unto them, bidding them to be of good comfort: For, said he, I have repented of my sins, and have been redeemed of the Lord; behold I am born of the Spirit.

"And the Lord said unto me: Marvel not that all mankind, yea, men and women, all nations, kindreds, tongues and people, must be born again; yea, born of God, changed from their carnal and fallen state, to a state of righteousness, being redeemed of God, becoming his sons and daughters; and thus they become new creatures; and unless they do this, they can in nowise inherit the kingdom of God.

"I say unto you, unless this be the case, they must be cast off; and this I know, because I was like to be cast off. Nevertheless, after wading through much tribulation, repenting nigh unto death, the Lord in mercy hath seen fit to snatch me out of an everlasting burning, and I am born of God.

"My soul hath been redeemed from the gall of bitterness and bonds of iniquity. I was in the darkest abyss; but now I behold the marvelous light of God. My soul was racked with eternal torment; but I am snatched, and my soul is pained no more.

"I rejected my Redeemer, and denied that which had been spoken of by our fathers; but now that they may foresee that he will come, and that he remembereth every creature of his creating, he will make himself manifest unto all.

"Yea, every knee shall bow, and every tongue confess before him. Yea, even at the last day, when all men shall stand to be judged of him, then shall they confess that he is God; then shall they confess, who live without God in the world, that the judgment of an everlasting punishment is just upon them; and they shall quake, and tremble, and shrink beneath the glance of his all-searching eye."

Having had this miraculous conversion, young Alma sought to confess his sins to the people he had misled in an attempt to reclaim them.

"And now it came to pass that Alma began from this time forward to teach the people, and those who were with Alma at the time the angel appeared unto them, traveling round about through all the land, publishing to all the people the things which they had heard and seen, and preaching the word of God in much tribulation, being greatly persecuted by those who were unbelievers, being smitten by many of them.

"But notwithstanding all this, they did impart much consolation to the church, confirming their faith, and exhorting them with long-suffering and much travail to keep the commandments of God.

"And four of them were the sons of Mosiah; and their names were Ammon, and Aaron, and Omner, and Himni; these were the names of the sons of Mosiah.

"And they traveled throughout all the land of Zarahemla, and among all the people who were under the reign of king Mosiah, zealously striving to repair all the injuries which they had done to the church, confessing all their sins, and publishing all the things which they had seen, and explaining the prophecies and the scriptures to all who desired to hear them.

"And thus they were instruments in the hands of God in bringing many to the knowledge of the truth, yea, to the knowledge of their Redeemer.

"And how blessed are they! For they did publish peace; they did publish good tidings of good; and they did declare unto the people that the Lord reigneth." (Mosiah 27:23-37.)

The sons of Mosiah were with Alma when the angel appeared. It was they who carried him, unconscious, to his father. The whole experience convinced them of their own wrongful life, and they, too, were converted to Christ, seeking as earnestly as did Alma to repair the damage they had done to the church.

Chapter 3

THEY PART COMPANY

Alma the younger became a good citizen and went into the ministry with his father, later succeeding him as high priest and head of the church.

It was different with the sons of Mosiah, although they were just as repentant as was Alma. They were offered the opportunity to help govern the kingdom, but they refused. As sons of the king, they were in line to succeed him on the throne, but their thoughts were turned in other directions. They had a deep desire to become missionaries to the Lamanites, and they had three things in mind. First, they desired to further show the Lord the depth of their repentance. Second, they humbly desired to bring salvation to the Lamanites as children of God. Third, they felt that to bring the Lamanites to a knowledge of Christ would also end the frequent wars they waged against the Nephites.

Mosiah believed that the time was near when he should retire from government and confer the crown upon one of his sons. Altogether he reigned for thirty-three years, having come to the throne when he was only thirty.* He had been faithful to God all his life and protected the church always. He was fair in his administration and did not lay heavy taxes upon the people. Like King Benjamin, his father, he worked for his own living.

Wishing to know the feelings of his people, Mosiah "sent out throughout all the land, among all the people, desiring to know their will concerning who should be their king.

"And it came to pass that the voice of the people came, saying: We are desirous that Aaron thy son should be our king and our ruler.

---

*Mosiah and Alma both died in 91 B.C., Mosiah at age sixty-three and Alma at age eighty-two. Some 509 years had elapsed since Lehi had left Jerusalem. (See Mosiah 29:45-46.)

"Now Aaron had gone up to the land of Nephi, therefore the king could not confer the kingdom upon him; neither would Aaron take upon him the kingdom; neither were any of the sons of Mosiah willing to take upon them the kingdom.

"Therefore king Mosiah sent again among the people; yea, even a written word sent he among the people. And these were the words that were written, saying: Behold, O ye my people, or my brethren, for I esteem you as such, I desire that ye should consider the cause which ye are called to consider—for ye are desirous to have a king. Now I declare unto you that he to whom the kingdom doth rightly belong has declined, and will not take upon him the kingdom.

"And now if there should be another appointed in his stead, behold I fear there would rise contentions among you. And who knoweth but what my son, to whom the kingdom doth belong, should turn to be angry and draw away a part of this people after him, which would cause wars and contentions among you, which would be the cause of shedding much blood and perverting the way of the Lord, yea, and destroy the souls of many people.

"Now I say unto you let us be wise and consider these things, for we have no right to destroy my son, neither should we have any right to destroy another if he should be appointed in his stead.

"And if my son should turn again to his pride and vain things he would recall the things which he had said, and claim his right to the kingdom, which would cause him and also this people to commit much sin.

"And now let us be wise and look forward to these things, and do that which will make for the peace of this people."

He therefore proposed to them a government of the people by themselves, saying, "Therefore I will be your king the remainder of my days; nevertheless, let us appoint judges, to judge this people according to our law; and we will newly arrange the affairs of this people, for we will appoint wise men to be judges, that will judge this people according to the commandments of God. Now it is better that a man should be judged of God than of man, for the judgments of God are always just, but the judgments of man are not always just.

"Therefore, if it were possible that you could have just men to be your kings, who would establish the laws of God, and judge this people according to his commandments, yea, if ye could have men for your kings who would do even as my father Benjamin did for this people—I say unto you, if this could always be the case then it would be expedient that ye should always have kings to rule over you.

"And even I myself have labored with all the power and faculties which I have possessed, to teach you the commandments of God, and to establish peace throughout the land, that there should be no wars nor contentions, no stealing, nor plundering, nor murdering, nor any manner of iniquity; and whosoever has committed iniquity, him have I punished according to the crime which he has committed, according to the law which has been given to us by our fathers.

"Now I say unto you, that because all men are not just it is not expedient that ye should have a king or kings to rule over you. For behold, how much iniquity doth one wicked king cause to be committed, yea, and what great destruction!

"Yea, remember king Noah, his wickedness and his abominations, and also the wickedness and abominations of his people. Behold what great destruction did come upon them; and also because of their iniquities they were brought into bondage.

"And were it not for the interposition of their all-wise Creator, and this because of their sincere repentance, they must unavoidably remain in bondage until now. But behold, he did deliver them because they did humble themselves before him; and because they cried mightily unto him he did deliver them out of bondage; and thus doth the Lord work with his power in all cases among the children of men, extending the arm of mercy towards them that put their trust in him.

"And behold, now I say unto you, ye cannot dethrone an iniquitous king save it be through much contention, and the shedding of much blood.

"For behold, he has his friends in iniquity, and he keepeth his guards about him; and he teareth up the laws of those who have reigned in righteousness before him; and he trampleth under his feet the commandments of God; and he enacteth laws, and sendeth them forth among his people, yea, laws after the manner of his own wickedness; and whosoever doth not obey his laws he causeth to be destroyed; and whosoever doth rebel against him he will send his armies against them to war, and if he can he will destroy them; and thus an unrighteous king doth pervert the ways of all righteousness.

"And now behold I say unto you, it is not expedient that such abominations should come upon you. Therefore, choose you by the voice of this people, judges, that ye may be judged according to the laws which have been given you by our fathers, which are correct, and which were given them by the hand of the Lord.

"Now it is not common that the voice of the people desireth anything contrary to that which is right; but it is common for the lesser part of the people to desire that which is not right; therefore this shall ye observe and make it your law—to do your business by the voice of the people.

"And if the time comes that the voice of the people doth choose iniquity, then is the time that the judgments of God will come upon you; yea, then is the time he will visit you with great destruction even as he has hitherto visited this land.

"And now if ye have judges, and they do not judge you according to the law which has been given, ye can cause that they may be judged of a higher judge. If your higher judges do not judge righteous judgments, ye shall cause that a small number of your lower judges should be gathered together, and they shall judge your higher judges, according to the voice of the people."

Mosiah now cautioned his people to preserve their country as a "land of liberty, and every man may enjoy his rights and privileges alike, so long as the Lord sees fit that we may live and inherit the land, yea, even as long as any of our posterity remains upon the face of the land."

So earnest was he that he added: "And I command you to do these things in the fear of the Lord; and I command you to do these things, and that ye have no king; that if these people commit sins and iniquities they shall be answered upon their own heads.

"For behold I say unto you, the sins of many people have been caused by the iniquities of their kings; therefore their iniquities are answered upon the heads of their kings."

He pointed further to evils that wicked kings could bring upon a nation: "Yea, all his iniquities and abominations, and all the wars, and contentions, and bloodshed, and the stealing, and the plundering, and the committing of whoredoms, and all manner of iniquities which cannot be enumerated—telling them that these things ought not to be, that they were expressly repugnant to the commandments of God."

The people were convinced by Mosiah's words. "Therefore they relinquished their desires for a king, and became exceedingly anxious that every man should have an equal chance throughout all the land; yea, and every man expressed a willingness to answer for his own sins.

"Therefore, it came to pass that they assembled themselves together in bodies throughout the land, to cast in their voices concerning who should be their judges, to judge them according to the law which had been given them; and they were exceedingly rejoiced because of the liberty which had been granted unto them.

"And they did wax strong in love towards Mosiah; yea, they did esteem him more than any other man; for they did not look upon him as a tyrant who was seeking for gain, yea, for that lucre which doth corrupt the soul; for he had not exacted riches of them, neither had he delighted in the shedding of blood; but he had established peace in the land, and he had granted unto his people that they should be delivered from all manner of bondage; therefore they did esteem him, yea, exceedingly, beyond measure.

"And it came to pass that they did appoint judges to rule over them, or to judge them according to the law; and this they did throughout all the land."

In the process, Alma the younger became the first chief judge in the new government. Already he was the high priest, "his father having conferred the office upon him, and having given him the charge concerning all the affairs of the church.

"And now it came to pass that Alma did walk in the ways of the Lord, and he did keep his commandments, and he did judge righteous judgments; and there was continual peace through the land.

"And thus commenced the reign of the judges throughout all the land of Zarahemla, among all the people who were called the Nephites; and Alma was the first and chief judge." (Mosiah 29.)

The king's four sons were given no place in the government at this time, nor in the church, because they had other plans.

Chapter 4

THEY SEEK
A MISSION

After their efforts to repair the damage done to the church in their sinful days, the sons of Mosiah desired to serve a mission to the Lamanites. These four young men—whose names were Ammon, Aaron, Omner, and Himni (Mosiah 27:34)—particularly wanted to go to the land of Nephi, now occupied by Lamanites but formerly the home of the Nephites.

They "returned to their father, the king, and desired of him that he would grant unto them that they might, with these whom they had selected, go up to the land of Nephi that they might preach the things which they had heard, and that they might impart the word of God to their brethren, the Lamanites—

"That perhaps they might bring them to the knowledge of the Lord their God, and convince them of the iniquity of their fathers; and that perhaps they might cure them of their hatred towards the Nephites, that they might also be brought to rejoice in the Lord their God, that they might become friendly to one another, and that there should be no more contentions in all the land which the Lord their God had given them.

"Now they were desirous that salvation should be declared to every creature, for they could not bear that any human soul should perish; yea, even the very thoughts that any soul should endure endless torment did cause them to quake and tremble."

The record says that "thus did the Spirit of the Lord work upon them, for they were the very vilest of sinners. And the Lord saw fit in his infinite mercy to spare them; nevertheless they suffered much anguish of soul because of their iniquities, suffering much and fearing that they should be cast off forever.

"And it came to pass that they did plead with their father many days that they might go up to the land of Nephi."

Remembering full well their past deeds, and not knowing if the Lord would accept them as missionaries, Mosiah knew he must seek permission. Would God approve of this mission? Would he guide Mosiah's sons and protect them and help them to convert these Lamanites, who had been so hostile to the Nephites?

"And king Mosiah went and inquired of the Lord if he should let his sons go up among the Lamanites to preach the word.

"And the Lord said unto Mosiah: Let them go up, for many shall believe on their words, and they shall have eternal life; and I will deliver thy sons out of the hands of the Lamanites.

"And it came to pass that Mosiah granted that they might go and do according to their request."

The young men then departed and went into the wilderness to begin their missionary work.

With his sons gone, Mosiah now turned to some ancient records that had been brought to him. They were engraved on gold plates in a language not understood by his people. (Mosiah 28:1-11.)

A group of Nephites who were known as the people of Limhi lived in another part of the country. They had no idea how to reach Zarahemla, but they wished to come and live there. They sent out an expedition to seek the way, but without success.

They did discover a land in which still another people had died in a great battle. Among the relics of this battle were records engraved on twenty-four gold plates. When they finally found their way to Zarahemla, they gave these records to King Mosiah, knowing that he was a prophet as well as a king and that he had the power to translate from unknown tongues. (See Mosiah 8:7-13; 22:11-14.)

"Now after Mosiah had finished translating these records, behold, it gave an account of the people who were destroyed, from the time that they were destroyed back to the building of the great tower, at the time the Lord confounded the language of the people and they were scattered abroad upon the face of all the earth, yea, and even from that time back until the creation of Adam.

"Now this account did cause the people of Mosiah to mourn exceedingly, yea, they were filled with sorrow; nevertheless it gave them much knowledge, in the which they did rejoice."

Feeling that he was near the end of his life, Mosiah now gave to Alma these plates, the brass plates of Laban, and all other records that had accumulated, as well as the Urim and Thummim by which the Lord allowed him to interpret strange languages.

Mosiah commanded Alma to "keep and preserve [the records], and also keep a record of the people, handing them down from one generation to another, even as they had been handed down from the time that Lehi left Jerusalem." (Mosiah 28:17-20.)

Chapter 5

THE MISSION BEGINS

A transformation very similar to the change of heart that came to Alma following his encounter with the angel also changed the sons of Mosiah.

"They had waxed strong in the knowledge of the truth; for they were men of a sound understanding and they had searched the scriptures diligently, that they might know the word of God.

"But this is not all; they had given themselves to much prayer, and fasting; therefore they had the spirit of prophecy, and the spirit of revelation, and when they taught, they taught with power and authority of God. . . .

"Having taken leave of their father, Mosiah, in the first year of the judges; having refused the kingdom which their father was desirous to confer upon them, and also this was the minds of the people; nevertheless they departed out of the land of Zarahemla, and took their swords, and their spears, and their bows, and their arrows, and their slings; and this they did that they might provide food for themselves while in the wilderness.

"And thus they departed into the wilderness with their numbers which they had selected, to go up to the land of Nephi, to preach the word of God unto the Lamanites.

"And it came to pass that they journeyed many days in the wilderness, and they fasted much and prayed much that the Lord would grant unto them a portion of his Spirit to go with them, and abide with them, that they might be an instrument in the hands of God to bring, if it were possible, their brethren, the Lamanites, to the knowledge of the truth, to the knowledge of the baseness of the traditions of their fathers, which were not correct.

"And it came to pass that the Lord did visit them with his Spirit, and said unto them: Be comforted. And they were comforted.

"And the Lord said unto them also: Go forth among the Lamanites, thy brethren, and establish my word; yet ye shall be patient in long-suffering and afflictions, that ye may show forth good examples unto them in me, and I will make an instrument of thee in my hands unto the salvation of many souls.

"And it came to pass that the hearts of the sons of Mosiah, and also those who were with them, took courage to go forth unto the Lamanites to declare unto them the word of God."

When they reached the borders of the Lamanites, they decided to separate and each go to a different part of the country, trusting the Lord to guide and protect them. "They supposed that great was the work which they had undertaken."

They realized that their efforts were to be directed toward "a wild and a hardened and a ferocious people; a people who delighted in murdering the Nephites, and robbing and plundering them; and their hearts were set upon riches, or upon gold and silver, and precious stones; yet they sought to obtain these things by murdering and plundering, that they might not labor for them with their own hands.

"Thus they were a very indolent people, many of whom did worship idols, and the curse of God had fallen upon them because of the traditions of their fathers; notwithstanding the promises of the Lord were extended unto them on the conditions of repentance.

"Therefore, this was the cause for which the sons of Mosiah had undertaken the work, that perhaps they might bring them unto repentance; that perhaps they might bring them to know of the plan of redemption.

"Therefore they separated themselves one from another, and went forth among them, every man alone, according to the word and power of God which was given unto him."

Little did they know the trials that awaited them for "they

did suffer much, both in body and in mind, such as hunger, thirst and fatigue, and also much labor in the spirit." (Alma 17:1-17.)

However, these brave young men had full confidence in the Lord, remembering that Mosiah had received assurance by revelation that their lives would be spared. The promise was, "Let them go up, for many shall believe on their words, and they shall have eternal life; and I will deliver thy sons out of the hands of the Lamanites." (Mosiah 28:7.)

Chapter 6

AMMON AND LAMONI

Before the missionaries separated for their various fields of labor, Ammon, their leader, blessed them and counseled further with them about the gospel principles they were to teach. Then, leaving his brothers, Ammon went directly to a land called Ishmael, where he was promptly seized by the Lamanite guards. He did not know that the king was temporarily outside the security area or that it was some of the alert royal guards who took him captive.

Ammon was tied securely and taken before the king, whose name was Lamoni. When intruders into the land had been caught previously, they were taken before the king, whose pleasure it was either to kill them, make slaves of them, put them in prison, or banish them from the area.

The king asked Ammon why he had come there and if it was his desire to live among his people.

"Yea, I desire to dwell among this people for a time," Ammon replied, "yea, and perhaps until the day I die."

Lamoni, who was greatly pleased with Ammon, ordered the guards to remove the ropes that bound him. Without any more knowledge of Ammon, and evidently being willing to let him live there, the king offered to give one of his daughters to Ammon as his wife.

"But Ammon said unto him: Nay, but I will be thy servant. Therefore Ammon became a servant to king Lamoni. And it came to pass that he was set among other servants to watch the flocks of Lamoni, according to the custom of the Lamanites.

"And after he had been in the service of the king three days, as he was with the Lamanitish servants going forth with their flocks to the place of water, which was called the water of

Sebus, and all the Lamanites drive their flocks hither, that they may have water—therefore, as Ammon and the servants of the king were driving forth their flocks to this place of water, behold, a certain number of the Lamanites, who had been with their flocks to water, stood and scattered the flocks of Ammon and the servants of the king, and they scattered them insomuch that they fled many ways."

The king previously had slain some of his servants who had allowed the sheep to be scattered. The men with Ammon now feared that they, too, would be killed for the same reason.

But Ammon saw here an opportunity to show the power of the Lord in protecting the king's flock. He said to the other servants, "My brethren, be of good cheer and let us go in search of the flocks, and we will gather them together and bring them back unto the place of water; and thus we will preserve the flocks unto the king and he will not slay us."

His companions brought the sheep back to the watering place while Ammon faced the intruders.

"And those men again stood to scatter their flocks; but Ammon said unto his brethren: Encircle the flocks round about that they flee not; and I go and contend with these men who do scatter our flocks.

"Therefore, they did as Ammon commanded them, and he went forth and stood to contend with those who stood by the waters of Sebus; and they were in number not a few."

Because the Lamanite intruders outnumbered Ammon, they did not fear him, believing that any one of their men could kill him. They could not know, of course, that the Lord would deliver His servant.

Ammon "began to cast stones at them with his sling; yea, with mighty power he did sling stones amongst them; and thus he slew a certain number of them insomuch that they began to be astonished at his power; nevertheless they were angry because of the slain of their brethren, and they were determined that he should fall; therefore, seeing that they could not hit him with their stones, they came forth with clubs to slay him.

"But behold, every man that lifted his club to smite Ammon, he smote off their arms with his sword; for he did withstand their blows by smiting their arms with the edge of his sword, insomuch that they began to be astonished, and began to flee before him; yea, and they were not few in number; and he caused them to flee by the strength of his arm."

Six were knocked down by Ammon's sling shots. When their leader attacked him with the sword, Ammon drew his own weapon and killed him. Others who now came against him with clubs found they were no match for him, for as they raised their arms to strike him, he cut off their arms with blows from his sword.

"And when he had driven them afar off, he returned and they watered their flocks and returned them to the pasture of the king, and then went in unto the king, bearing the arms which had been smitten off by the sword of Ammon, of those who sought to slay him; and they were carried in unto the king for a testimony of the things which they had done." (Alma 17:18-39.)

The servants told the king all that had happened. Frightened, he said, "Surely, this is more than a man. Behold, is not this the Great Spirit who doth send such great punishments upon this people, because of their murders?

"And they answered the king, and said: Whether he be the Great Spirit or a man, we know not; but this much we do know, that he cannot be slain by the enemies of the king; neither can they scatter the king's flocks when he is with us, because of his expertness and great strength; therefore, we know that he is a friend to the king. And now, O king, we do not believe that a man has such great power, for we know he cannot be slain.

"And now, when the king heard these words, he said unto them: Now I know that it is the Great Spirit; and he has come down at this time to preserve your lives, that I might not slay you as I did your brethren. Now this is the Great Spirit of whom our fathers have spoken.

"Now this was the tradition of Lamoni, which he had received from his father, that there was a Great Spirit. Notwithstanding they believed in a Great Spirit, they supposed that whatsoever they did was right; nevertheless, Lamoni began to fear exceedingly, with fear lest he had done wrong in slaying his servants."

One thing Lamoni feared was that the Great Spirit would now punish him for killing other servants who had allowed the sheep to be scattered.

Lamoni asked his servants where Ammon was. "And they said unto him: Behold, he is feeding thy horses. Now the king had commanded his servants, previous to the time of the watering of their flocks, that they should prepare his horses and chariots, and conduct him forth to the land of Nephi; for there had been a great feast appointed at the land of Nephi, by the father of Lamoni, who was king over all the land.

"Now when king Lamoni heard that Ammon was preparing his horses and his chariots he was more astonished, because of the faithfulness of Ammon, saying: Surely there has not been any servant among all my servants that has been so faithful as this man; for even he doth remember all my commandments to execute them. Now I surely know that this is the Great Spirit, and I would desire him that he come in unto me, but I durst not."

When Ammon came at the king's call, he asked, "What wilt thou that I should do for thee, O king? And the king answered him not for the space of an hour, according to their time, for he knew not what he should say unto him."

The king was so frightened that he could not talk, so Ammon repeated his question. The king still did not answer.

"And it came to pass that Ammon, being filled with the Spirit of God, therefore he perceived the thoughts of the king. And he said unto him: Is it because thou hast heard that I defended thy servants and thy flocks, and slew seven of their brethren with the sling and with the sword, and smote off the arms of others, in order to defend thy flocks and thy servants; behold, is it this that causeth thy marvelings? I say unto you, what is it, that thy marvelings are so great? Behold, I am a man, and am thy servant; therefore, whatsoever thou desirest which is right, that will I do."

Lamoni then asked Ammon who he was. "Art thou that Great Spirit, who knows all things?

"Ammon answered and said unto him: I am not.

"And the king said: How knowest thou the thoughts of my heart? Thou mayest speak boldly, and tell me concerning these things; and also tell me by what power ye slew and smote off the arms of my brethren that scattered my flocks—and now, if thou wilt tell me concerning these things, whatsoever thou desirest I will give unto thee; and if it were needed, I would guard thee with my armies; but I know that thou art more powerful than all they; nevertheless, whatsoever thou desirest of me I will grant it unto thee."

Ammon then asked, "Wilt thou hearken unto my words, if I tell thee by what power I do these things? And this is the thing that I desire of thee."

The king replied, "Yea, I will believe all thy words."

Ammon boldly began to teach the king. He asked Lamoni, "Believest thou that there is a God?"

Lamoni answered, "I do not know what that meaneth."

"Believest thou that there is a Great Spirit?"

"Yea."

Ammon told him, "This is God." Then he asked again, "Believest thou that this Great Spirit, who is God, created all things which are in heaven and in the earth?"

Lamoni said, "Yea, I believe that he created all things which are in the earth; but I do not know the heavens."

"The heavens is a place where God dwells and all his holy angels," Alma explained.

"Is it above the earth?" Lamoni asked.

"Yea, and he looketh down upon all the children of men; and he knows all the thoughts and intents of the heart; for by his hand were they all created from the beginning."

Then King Lamoni said, "I believe all these things which thou hast spoken. Art thou sent from God?" (Alma 18:1-33.)

Chapter 7

THE KING
IS CONVERTED

When King Lamoni asked Ammon if he were sent from God, Ammon replied:

"I am a man; and man in the beginning was created after the image of God, and I am called by his Holy Spirit to teach these things unto this people, that they may be brought to a knowledge of that which is just and true; and a portion of that Spirit dwelleth in me, which giveth me knowledge, and also power according to my faith and desires which are in God.

"Now when Ammon had said these words, he began at the creation of the world, and also the creation of Adam, and told him all the things concerning the fall of man, and rehearsed and laid before him the records and the holy scriptures of the people, which had been spoken by the prophets, even down to the time that their father, Lehi, left Jerusalem."

He told Lamoni and his servants of Lehi's coming from Jerusalem with his family and of their difficult journey.

"And he also rehearsed unto them concerning the rebellions of Laman and Lemuel, and the sons of Ishmael, yea, all their rebellions did he relate unto them; and he expounded unto them all the records and scriptures from the time that Lehi left Jerusalem down to the present time.

"But this is not all; for he expounded unto them the plan of redemption, which was prepared from the foundation of the world; and he also made known unto them concerning the coming of Christ, and all the works of the Lord did he make known unto them.

"And it came to pass that after he had said all these things, and expounded them to the king, that the king believed all his words. And he began to cry unto the Lord, saying: O Lord, have mercy; according to thy abundant mercy which thou hast had upon the people of Nephi, have upon me, and my people."

Suddenly the king was overpowered by the Holy Spirit and fell to the earth as if he had died. His awestruck servants carried him to his bed in the palace, thinking he was dead. They called the queen and her children, all of whom mourned for two days and two nights while he lay motionless. (Alma 18:34-43.)

The attendants at the palace urged that the king be buried, being convinced of his death. But the queen would not agree. She had heard of Ammon and the great things he had done, and now she sent for him.

When Ammon was brought before her, the queen said, "The servants of my husband have made it known unto me that thou art a prophet of a holy God, and that thou hast power to do many mighty works in his name; therefore, if this is the case, I would that ye should go in and see my husband, for he has been laid upon his bed for the space of two days and two nights; and some say that he is not dead, but others say that he is dead and that he stinketh, and that he ought to be placed in the sepulchre; but as for myself, to me he doth not stink."

This was the opportunity Ammon desired, for "he knew that king Lamoni was under the power of God; he knew that the dark veil of unbelief was being cast away from his mind, and the light which did light up his mind, which was the light of the glory of God, which was a marvelous light of his goodness—yea, this light had infused such joy into his soul, the cloud of darkness having been dispelled, and that the light of everlasting life was lit up in his soul, yea, he knew that this had overcome his natural frame, and he was carried away in God—therefore, what the queen desired of him was his only desire. Therefore, he went in to see the king according as the queen had desired him; and he saw the king, and he knew that he was not dead.

"And he said unto the queen: He is not dead, but he sleepeth in God, and on the morrow he shall rise again; therefore bury him not.

"And Ammon said unto her: Believest thou this? And she said unto him: I have had no witness save thy word, and the word of our servants; nevertheless I believe that it shall be according as thou hast said.

"And Ammon said unto her: Blessed art thou because of thy exceeding faith; I say unto thee, woman, there has not been such great faith among all the people of the Nephites."

The queen continued to watch over her husband until the next day, when Ammon promised that he would waken.

According to the promise, the king arose and "stretched forth his hand unto the woman, and said: Blessed be the name of God, and blessed art thou. For as sure as thou livest, behold, I have seen my Redeemer; and he shall come forth, and be born of a woman, and he shall redeem all mankind who believe on his name. Now, when he had said these words, his heart was swollen within him, and he sunk again with joy; and the queen also sunk down, being overpowered by the Spirit."

Ammon now realized that his prayers in behalf of these people had been fulfilled. He knelt again to the Lord "and began to pour out his soul in prayer and thanksgiving to God for what he had done for his brethren; and he was also overpowered with joy; and thus they all three had sunk to the earth."

When the servants in the palace saw this, they too began to pray, "for the fear of the Lord had come upon them also, for it was they who had stood before the king and testified unto him concerning the great power of Ammon.

"And it came to pass that they did call on the name of the Lord, in their might, even until they had all fallen to the earth, save it were one of the Lamanitish women, whose name was Abish, she having been converted unto the Lord for many years, on account of a remarkable vision of her father—

"Thus, having been converted to the Lord, and never having made it known, therefore, when she saw that all the servants of Lamoni had fallen to the earth, and also her mistress, the queen, and the king, and Ammon lay prostrate upon the earth, she knew that it was the power of God; and supposing that this opportunity, by making known unto the people what had happened among them, that by beholding this scene it would cause them to believe in the power of God, therefore she ran forth from house to house, making it known unto the people."

As the people assembled in the palace and saw the king and the queen prostrate and seemingly lifeless, they thought a "great evil" had been brought upon the king's family because he had allowed a Nephite to live in the land.

Some of the men who scattered the sheep were there too, and, recognizing Ammon, they became very angry. One of them, whose brother had been slain with the sword of Ammon, being exceedingly angry with Ammon, drew his sword and went forth that he might let it fall upon Ammon, to slay him; and as he lifted the sword to smite him, behold, he fell dead."

The Lord was keeping his promise to protect Mosiah's sons.

"And it came to pass that when the multitude beheld that the man had fallen dead, who lifted the sword to slay Ammon, fear came upon them all, and they durst not put forth their hands to touch him or any of those who had fallen; and they began to marvel again among themselves what could be the cause of this great power, or what all these things could mean."

Some of the people thought Ammon really was the Great Spirit. Others said he was sent by the Great Spirit to afflict them because of their wicked lives.

"And thus the contention began to be exceedingly sharp among them. And while they were thus contending, the woman servant who had caused the multitude to be gathered together came, and when she saw the contention which was among the multitude she was exceedingly sorrowful, even unto tears.

"And it came to pass that she went and took the queen by the hand, that perhaps she might raise her from the ground; and as soon as she touched her hand she arose and stood upon her feet, and cried with a loud voice, saying: O blessed Jesus, who has saved me from an awful hell! O blessed God, have mercy on this people!

"And when she had said this, she clasped her hands, being

filled with joy, speaking many words which were not understood; and when she had done this, she took the king, Lamoni, by the hand, and behold he arose and stood upon his feet.

"And he, immediately, seeing the contention among his people, went forth and began to rebuke them, and to teach them the words which he had heard from the mouth of Ammon; and as many as heard his words believed, and were converted unto the Lord.

"But there were many among them who would not hear his words; therefore they went their way."

When they all arose "they did all declare unto the people the selfsame thing—that their hearts had been changed; that they had no more desire to do evil.

"And behold, many did declare unto the people that they had seen angels and had conversed with them; and thus they had told them things of God, and of his righteousness."

Many Lamanites were converted by these events and "were baptized; and they became a righteous people, and they did establish a church among them.

"And thus the work of the Lord did commence among the Lamanites; thus the Lord did begin to pour out his Spirit upon them; and we see that his arm is extended to all people who will repent and believe on his name." (Alma 19.)

Chapter 8

LAMONI'S FATHER IS SPARED

 King Lamoni reigned over the land of Ishmael, which was only a part of the domain of the Lamanites. His father was king over the entire region, and Lamoni served under him.

After Ammon had established the church in Ishmael, Lamoni asked him to accompany him to the capital city of the entire land, so that his father, the chief king, could come to know him.

But "the voice of the Lord came to Ammon, saying: Thou shalt not go up to the land of Nephi, for behold, the king will seek thy life; but thou shalt go to the land of Middoni; for behold, thy brother Aaron, and also Muloki and Ammah are in prison."

Upon receiving this revelation, Ammon told Lamoni, "My brother and brethren are in prison at Middoni, and I go that I may deliver them."

Lamoni, now a loyal friend of Ammon, declared, "I know, in the strength of the Lord thou canst do all things. But behold, I will go with thee to the land of Middoni; for the king of the land of Middoni, whose name is Antiomno, is a friend unto me; therefore I go to the land of Middoni, that I may flatter the king of the land, and he will cast thy brethren out of prison. Now Lamoni said unto him: Who told thee that thy brethren were in prison?

"And Ammon said unto him: No one hath told me, save it be God; and he said unto me—Go and deliver thy brethren, for they are in prison in the land of Middoni."

Lamoni ordered his servants to make the horses and chariots ready. Then he said to Ammon, "Come, I will go with thee

down to the land of Middoni, and there I will plead with the king
that he will cast thy brethren out of prison."

As they traveled, they met Lamoni's father on the highway,
and they all stopped to greet each other.

The father said to his son: "Why did ye not come to the feast
on that great day when I made a feast unto my sons, and unto my
people? . . . Whither art thou going with this Nephite, who is
one of the children of a liar?"

Lamoni feared to offend his father, so he quickly explained
where he and Ammon were going. He also told him briefly of
the things that had happened since Ammon came into Ishmael.

"And now when Lamoni had rehearsed unto him all these
things, behold, to his astonishment, his father was angry with
him, and said: Lamoni, thou art going to deliver these Nephites,
who are sons of a liar. Behold, he robbed our fathers; and now
his children are also come amongst us that they may, by their
cunning and their lyings, deceive us, that they again may rob us
of our property.

"Now the father of Lamoni commanded him that he should
slay Ammon with the sword. And he also commanded him that
he should not go to the land of Middoni, but that he should return with him to the land of Ishmael.

"But Lamoni said unto him: I will not slay Ammon, neither
will I return to the land of Ishmael, but I go to the land of Middoni that I may release the brethren of Ammon, for I know that
they are just men and holy prophets of the true God."

So angry was the old king that he drew his sword to kill Lamoni, his own son. But Ammon quickly stepped forward and
said:

"Behold, thou shalt not slay thy son; nevertheless, it were
better that he should fall than thee, for behold, he has repented
of his sins; but if thou shouldst fall at this time, in thine anger,
thy soul could not be saved. And again, it is expedient that thou
shouldst forbear; for if thou shouldst slay thy son, he being an
innocent man, his blood would cry from the ground to the Lord

his God, for vengeance to come upon thee; and perhaps thou wouldst lose thy soul."

The old king replied, "I know that if I should slay my son, that I should shed innocent blood; for it is thou that hast sought to destroy him."

Then he rushed at Ammon with his sword, but Ammon retaliated and wounded the king in the arm so that he could no longer fight. The old king, seeing that he was at the mercy of Ammon, began to beg for his life.

"But Ammon raised his sword, and said unto him: Behold, I will smite thee except thou wilt grant unto me that my brethren may be cast out of prison.

"Now the king, fearing he should lose his life, said: If thou wilt spare me I will grant unto thee whatsoever thou wilt ask, even to half of the kingdom.

"Now when Ammon saw that he had wrought upon the old king according to his desire, he said unto him: If thou wilt grant that my brethren may be cast out of prison, and also that Lamoni may retain his kingdom, and that ye be not displeased with him, but grant that he may do according to his own desires in whatsoever thing he thinketh, then will I spare thee; otherwise I will smite thee to the earth.

"Now when Ammon had said these words, the king began to rejoice because of his life.

"And when he saw that Ammon had no desire to destroy him, and when he also saw the great love he had for his son Lamoni, he was astonished exceedingly, and said: Because this is all that thou hast desired, that I would release thy brethren, and suffer that my son Lamoni should retain his kingdom, behold, I will grant unto you that my son may retain his kingdom from this time and forever; and I will govern him no more—

"And I will also grant unto thee that thy brethren may be cast out of prison, and thou and thy brethren may come unto me, in my kingdom; for I shall greatly desire to see thee. For the king was greatly astonished at the words which he had spoken, and also at the words which had been spoken by his son Lamoni, therefore he was desirous to learn them."

Ammon and Lamoni now continued on their journey to the city of Middoni, where Ammon's brothers were held in prison.

"And Lamoni found favor in the eyes of the king of the land; therefore the brethren of Ammon were brought forth out of prison."

Ammon was shocked when he saw his brothers. They had suffered severe hardships and persecution. They were naked and had deep sores where the ropes that bound them had cut into their flesh. They also had experienced both hunger and thirst, but, the record says, through it all "they were patient in all their sufferings." They had "fallen into the hands of a more hardened and a more stiffnecked people" than had Ammon.

Driven out of city after city, they finally arrived in Middoni, where they were "bound with strong cords, and kept in prison for many days" until they were delivered by Lamoni and Ammon. (Alma 20.)

Chapter 9

THE JOURNEY
OF AARON

When Ammon and his brothers separated at the beginning of their missions to the Lamanites, Aaron went to a large city that the people named Jerusalem. Three different groups had joined in its construction—the Lamanites themselves, the Amalekites, and a third group known as the people of Amulon. All three groups continued to occupy the city. (Alma 21:1-2.)

The Amalekites, who were followers of a man named Amaleki, were among the most bitter apostates who had broken away from the Nephites. When they left the true church, they adopted the religion of a man named Nehor and went over to dwell with the Lamanites.

Nehor, a rebellious man who lived in the days of Alma, about 91 years B.C., first preached in the city where he lived. One day he met a faithful but elderly soldier of the Nephite army, named Gideon. When Gideon denounced Nehor's false doctrines, Nehor drew a sword and killed him. He was quickly arrested, tried for murder, and executed.

"Nevertheless, this did not put an end to the spreading of priestcraft through the land; for there were many who loved the vain things of the world, and they went forth preaching false doctrines; and this they did for the sake of riches and honor." (Alma 1:1-16.)

When Amaleki became an enemy to the Nephites, he adopted the religion of Nehor and built synagogues in which his followers practiced many false teachings. This apostate group flourished in several Nephite communities and then spread among the Lamanites. The bitterness of Amaleki's followers toward the Nephites was so strong that many of them wanted to raise an army and fight. It was this group that helped the Lamanites build the city of Jerusalem, which Aaron, as a missionary, now approached.

The other apostate group in the city was the Amulonites. They descended from one of the corrupt priests of the wicked King Noah, who had killed the prophet Abinadi.

When the Lamanites had come against King Noah, he and his entire group of priests had fled into the wilderness. Noah was killed, leaving the priests to themselves.

One day the priests saw a group of Lamanite girls dancing. They kidnapped the girls and took them to be their wives. The Amulonites were descended from this group and, therefore, were half-blooded Nephites and half Lamanites. However, their full allegiance was with the Lamanites.

"Now the Lamanites of themselves were sufficiently hardened, but the Amalekites and the Amulonites were still harder; therefore they did cause the Lamanites that they should harden their hearts, that they should wax strong in wickedness and their abominations." (Alma 21:3.)

When Aaron came to the city Jerusalem, he went to the synagogues of the followers of Nehor, where both the Amalekites and Amulonites worshipped. As he entered into one of the synagogues to preach one day, an Amalekite stood up and challenged him:

"What is that thou hast testified?" the Amalekite asked. "Hast thou seen an angel? Why do not angels appear unto us? Behold are not this people as good as thy people? Thou also sayest, except we repent we shall perish. How knowest thou the thoughts and intent of our hearts? How knowest thou that we have cause to repent? How knowest thou that we are not a righteous people? Behold, we have built sanctuaries, and we do assemble ourselves together to worship God. We do believe that God will save all men."

Aaron asked the man, "Believest thou that the Son of God shall come to redeem mankind from their sins?"

The man responded, "We do not believe that thou knowest

any such thing. We do not believe in these foolish traditions. We do not believe that thou knowest of things to come, neither do we believe that thy fathers and also that our fathers did know concerning the things which they spake, of that which is to come."

Aaron quoted the scriptures to the congregation, telling them of the coming of the Savior and the resurrection of the dead. He stressed that there could be no salvation for anyone except through the atonement of Christ. As he did so, the people became angry and mocked him, refusing any longer to listen.

"Therefore, when he saw that they would not hear his words, he departed out of their synagogue, and came over to a village which was called Ani-Anti, and there he found Muloki preaching the word unto them; and also Ammah and his brethren. And they contended with many about the word. And it came to pass that they saw that the people would harden their hearts, therefore they departed and came over into the land of Middoni. And they did preach the word unto many, and few believed on the words which they taught."

Aaron and his brothers, who had joined him, were put in prison, where they remained until Lamoni and Ammon rescued them.

Ammon and Lamoni then returned to the land of Ishmael, but Aaron and his brothers, now refreshed from their imprisonment, decided to continue with their missionary work. "And they went forth again to declare the word, and thus they were delivered for the first time out of prison; and thus they had suffered.

"And they went forth whithersoever they were led by the Spirit of the Lord, preaching the word of God in every synagogue of the Amalekites, or in every assembly of the Lamanites where they could be admitted.

"And it came to pass that the Lord began to bless them, insomuch that they brought many to the knowledge of the truth; yea, they did convince many of their sins, and of the traditions of their fathers, which were not correct." (Alma 21:3-17.)

Chapter 10

THE OLD KING IS CONVERTED

The Spirit directed Aaron to go to the land Nephi, where Lamoni's father, the old king, lived. This king controlled the entire region, except that he had now given Lamoni freedom to govern the land of Ishmael by himself.

Aaron went directly to the palace and was admitted to the throne room. Bowing low, he said: "Behold, O king, we are the brethren of Ammon, whom thou hast delivered out of prison. And now, O king, if thou wilt spare our lives, we will be thy servants."

The king replied: "Arise, for I will grant unto you your lives, and I will not suffer that ye shall be my servants; but I will insist that ye shall administer unto me; for I have been somewhat troubled in mind because of the generosity and the greatness of the words of thy brother Ammon; and I desire to know the cause why he has not come up out of Middoni with thee."

Aaron declared to the king that the Holy Spirit had directed Ammon to return with Lamoni to Ishmael.

The old king replied: "What is this that ye have said concerning the Spirit of the Lord? Behold, this is the thing which doth trouble me."

Aaron then told him of the Creation and how God formed Adam in His own image, and of the fall of Adam. He explained the redemption through the Savior, saying, "And since man had fallen he could not merit anything of himself; but the sufferings and death of Christ atone for their sins, through faith and repentance, and so forth; and that he breaketh the bands of death, that the grave shall have no victory, and that the sting of death should be swallowed up in the hopes of glory."

After Aaron had expounded these things, the king said, "What shall I do that I may have this eternal life of which thou hast spoken? Yea, what shall I do that I may be born of God, having this wicked spirit rooted out of my breast, and receive his Spirit, that I may be filled with joy, that I may not be cast off at the last day? Behold, said he, I will give up all that I possess, yea, I will forsake my kingdom, that I may receive this great joy."

Aaron told him, "If thou desirest this thing, if thou wilt bow down before God, yea, if thou wilt repent of all thy sins, and will bow down before God, and call on his name in faith, believing that ye shall receive, then shalt thou receive the hope which thou desirest."

The king knelt down in prayer, then prostrated himself completely and cried out, "O God, Aaron hath told me that there is a God; and if there is a God, and if thou art God, wilt thou make thyself known unto me, and I will give away all my sins to know thee, and that I may be raised from the dead, and be saved at the last day. And now when the king had said these words, he was struck as if he were dead."

The king's servants ran in great fear to call the queen.

"And she came in unto the king; and when she saw him lay as if he were dead, and also Aaron and his brethren standing as though they had been the cause of his fall, she was angry with them, and commanded that her servants, or the servants of the king, should take them and slay them.

"Now the servants had seen the cause of the king's fall, therefore they durst not lay their hands on Aaron and his brethren; and they pled with the queen saying: Why commandest thou that we should slay these men, when behold one of them is mightier than us all? Therefore we shall fall before them.

"Now when the queen saw the fear of the servants she also began to fear exceedingly, lest there should some evil come upon her. And she commanded her servants that they should go and call the people, that they might slay Aaron and his brethren."

Aaron, seeing the queen's determination, and also "knowing the hardness of the hearts of the people, feared lest that a multitude should assemble themselves together, and there should be a great contention and a disturbance among them; therefore he put forth his hand and raised the king from the earth, and said unto him: Stand. And he stood upon his feet, receiving his strength.

"Now this was done in the presence of the queen and many of the servants. And when they saw it they greatly marveled, and began to fear. And the king stood forth, and began to minister unto them. And he did minister unto them, insomuch that his whole household were converted unto the Lord."

The queen had directed the servants to call in other people, "and there began to be great murmurings among them because of Aaron and his brethren.

"But the king stood forth among them and administered unto them. And they were pacified towards Aaron and those who were with him.

"And it came to pass that when the king saw that the people were pacified, he caused that Aaron and his brethren should stand forth in the midst of the multitude, and that they should preach the word unto them." (Alma 22:1-26.)

Chapter 11

RELIGIOUS LIBERTY IS GRANTED

Following his conversion, the old king sent a proclamation throughout his kingdom announcing that Ammon, Aaron, Omner, and Himni were free to go anywhere in the land, preaching the gospel. He forbade that anyone should lay their hands on them.

"Yea, he sent a decree among them, that they should not lay their hands on them to bind them, or to cast them into prison; neither should they spit upon them, nor smite them, nor cast them out of their synagogues, nor scourge them; neither should they cast stones at them, but that they should have free access to their houses, and also their temples, and their sanctuaries.

"And thus they might go forth and preach the word according to their desires, for the king had been converted unto the Lord, and all his household; therefore he sent his proclamation throughout the land unto his people, that the word of God might have no obstruction, but that it might go forth throughout all the land, that his people might be convinced concerning the wicked traditions of their fathers, and that they might be convinced that they were all brethren, and that they ought not to murder, nor to plunder, nor to steal, nor to commit adultery, nor to commit any manner of wickedness."

Aaron and his brothers then went from "city to city, and from one house of worship to another, establishing churches, and consecrating priests and teachers throughout the land among the Lamanites, to preach and to teach the word of God among them; and thus they began to have great success.

"And thousands were brought to the knowledge of the Lord, yea, thousands were brought to believe in the traditions of the

Nephites; and they were taught the records and prophecies which were handed down even to the present time.

"And as sure as the Lord liveth, so sure as many as believed, or as many as were brought to the knowledge of the truth, through the preaching of Ammon and his brethren, according to the spirit of revelation and of prophecy, and the power of God working miracles in them—yea, I say unto you, as the Lord liveth, as many of the Lamanites as believed in their preaching, and were converted unto the Lord, never did fall away.

"For they became a righteous people; they did lay down the weapons of their rebellion, that they did not fight against God any more, neither against any of their brethren.

"Now, these are they who were converted unto the Lord: The people of the Lamanites who were in the land of Ishmael; and also of the people of the Lamanites who were in the land of Middoni; and also of the people of the Lamanites who were in the city of Nephi; and also of the people of the Lamanites who were in the land of Shilom, and who were in the land of Shemlon, and in the city of Lemuel, and in the city of Shimnilom.

"And these are the names of the cities of the Lamanites which were converted unto the Lord; and these are they that laid down the weapons of their rebellion, yea, all their weapons of war; and they were all Lamanites."

It was the Lamanites who accepted Christ. Only one Amalekite joined the church, and none of the Amulonites, for "they did harden their hearts, and also the hearts of the Lamanites in that part of the land wheresoever they dwelt, yea, and all their villages and all their cities."

The newly converted Lamanites wished to become a separate people by themselves, no longer associated with the Amalekites and Amulonites. The record explains:

"And now it came to pass that the king and those who were converted were desirous that they might have a name, that thereby they might be distinguished from their brethren; therefore the king consulted with Aaron and many of their priests, concerning the name that they should take upon them, that they might be distinguished.

"And it came to pass that they called their names Anti-Nephi-Lehies; and they were called by this name and were no more called Lamanites.

"And they began to be a very industrious people; yea, and they were friendly with the Nephites; therefore, they did open a correspondence with them, and the curse of God did no more follow them." (Alma 23.)

Chapter 12

THE THREAT OF WAR

The action of the believing Lamanites greatly angered the Amalekites and Amulonites.

"And their hatred became exceedingly sore against them, even insomuch that they began to rebel against their king, insomuch that they would not that he should be their king; therefore, they took up arms against the people of Anti-Nephi-Lehi.

"Now the king conferred the kingdom upon his son, and he called his name Anti-Nephi-Lehi. And the king died in that selfsame year that the Lamanites began to make preparations for war against the people of God."

Ammon and his brothers were deeply concerned. They met in the land of Midian "and from thence they came to the land of Ishmael that they might hold a council with Lamoni and also with this brother Anti-Nephi-Lehi, what they should do to defend themselves against the Lamanites."

The converted Lamanites determined not to take up arms, even in self-defense. The king addressed them, saying: "I thank my God, my beloved people, that our great God has in goodness sent these our brethren, the Nephites, unto us to preach unto us, and to convince us of the traditions of our wicked fathers.

"And behold, I thank my great God that he has given us a portion of his Spirit to soften our hearts, that we have opened a correspondence with these brethren, the Nephites.

"And behold, I also thank my God, that by opening this correspondence we have been convinced of our sins, and of the many murders which we have committed.

"And I also thank my God, yea, my great God, that he hath granted unto us that we might repent of these things, and also that he hath forgiven us of those our many sins and murders which we have committed, and taken away the guilt from our hearts, through the merits of his Son.

"And now behold, my brethren, since it has been all that we could do, (as we were the most lost of all mankind) to repent of all our sins and the many murders which we have committed, and to get God to take them away from our hearts, for it was all we could do to repent sufficiently before God that he would take away our stain—now, my best beloved brethren, since God hath taken away our stains, and our swords have become bright, then let us stain our swords no more with the blood of our brethren.

"Behold, I say unto you, Nay, let us retain our swords that they be not stained with the blood of our brethren; for perhaps, if we should stain our swords again they can no more be washed bright through the blood of the Son of our great God, which shall be shed for the atonement of our sins.

"And the great God has had mercy on us, and made these things known unto us that we might not perish; yea, and he has made these things known unto us beforehand, because he loveth our souls as well as he loveth our children; therefore, in his mercy he doth visit us by his angels, that the plan of salvation might be made known unto us as well as unto future generations.

"Oh, how merciful is our God! And now behold, since it has been as much as we could do to get our stains taken away from us, and our swords are made bright, let us hide them away that they may be kept bright, as a testimony to our God at the last day, or at the day that we shall be brought to stand before him to be judged, that we have not stained our swords in the blood of our brethren since he imparted his word unto us and has made us clean thereby.

"And now, my brethren, if our brethren seek to destroy us, behold, we will hide away our swords, yea, even we will bury them deep in the earth, that they may be kept bright, as a testimony that we have never used them, at the last day; and if our brethren destroy us, behold, we shall go to our God and shall be saved."

So it was that the people gathered together all their weapons and buried them "deep in the earth," as a testimony to God and man "that they never would use weapons again for the shedding of man's blood; and this they did, vouching and covenanting with God, that rather than shed the blood of their brethren they would give up their own lives; and rather than take away from a brother they would give unto him; and rather than spend their days in idleness they would labor abundantly with their hands."

Unbelieving Lamanites joined the other enemies of the converts and determined to kill the king and replace him with one of their own number. Their armies then marched to attack those who had joined the church. The converts, seeing the approaching soldiers, "went out to meet them, and prostrated themselves before them to the earth, and began to call on the name of the Lord; and thus they were in this attitude when the Lamanites began to fall upon them, and began to slay them with the sword. And thus without meeting any resistance, they did slay a thousand and five of them; and we know that they are blessed, for they have gone to dwell with their God."

When the Lamanites who made the attack saw that the converts would not resist them, they stopped their slaughter, "and there were many whose hearts had swollen in them for those of their brethren who had fallen under the sword, for they repented of the things which they had done.

"And it came to pass that they threw down their weapons of war, and they would not take them again, for they were stung for the murders which they had committed; and they came down even as their brethren, relying upon the mercies of those whose arms were lifted to slay them.

"And it came to pass that the people of God were joined that day by more than the number who had been slain; and those who had been slain were righteous people, therefore we have no reason to doubt but what they were saved.

"And there was not a wicked man slain among them; but

there were more than a thousand brought to the knowledge of the truth; thus we see that the Lord worketh in many ways to the salvation of his people.

"Now the greatest number of those of the Lamanites who slew so many of their brethren were Amalekites and Amulonites, the greatest number of whom were after the order of the Nehors."

No Amalekites or Amulonites joined the church following this great demonstration of faith, only Lamanites.

As Mormon wrote of this event, he commented on the effect of apostasy and said: "And thus we can plainly discern, that after a people have been once enlightened by the Spirit of God, and have had great knowledge of things pertaining to righteousness, and then have fallen away into sin and transgression, they become more hardened, and thus their state becomes worse than though they had never known these things." (Alma 24.)

Chapter 13

AGGRESSION SPREADS

The attacking Lamanites regretted killing people of their own race, especially since they offered no resistance. They left the Anti-Nephi-Lehi converts in peace, but swore vengeance on the Nephite nation for sending missionaries to work among them. They had brought about this great conversion.

Lamanite armies now attacked a Nephite city called Ammonihah. The people of Ammonihah were very corrupt. It was they who had been so cruel to the prophet Alma when he tried to preach to them. The armies destroyed the city and its entire population.

Later the Lamanite army attacked the Nephites near Zarahemla but were beaten back. Then Aaron's good work produced still further fruit. Many other Lamanites began to remember his words, and "therefore they began to disbelieve the traditions of their fathers, and to believe in the Lord, and that he gave great power unto the Nephites; and thus there were many of them converted in the wilderness."

The Amulonites, however, caused many of the new converts to be put to death in the wilderness. This angered the Lamanites greatly, "and the Lamanites began to hunt the seed of Amulon and his brethren and began to slay them; and . . . they are hunted at this day by the Lamanites."

Finally, the remaining Lamanites returned to their own land. "Many of them came over to dwell in the land of Ishmael and the land of Nephi, and did join themselves to the people of God, who were the people of Anti-Nephi-Lehi.

"And they did also bury their weapons of war, according as their brethren had, and they began to be a righteous people; and they did walk in the ways of the Lord, and did observe to keep his commandments and his statutes.

"Yea, and they did keep the law of Moses; for it was expedient that they should keep the law of Moses as yet, for it was not all fulfilled. But notwithstanding the law of Moses, they did look forward to the coming of Christ, considering that the law of Moses was a type of his coming, and believing that they must keep those outward performances until the time that he should be revealed unto them.

"Now they did not suppose that salvation came by the law of Moses; but the law of Moses did serve to strengthen their faith in Christ; and thus they did retain a hope through faith, unto eternal salvation, relying upon the spirit of prophecy, which spake of those things to come." (Alma 25.)

Ammon and his brethren rejoiced over this. Ammon was so thrilled that he declared: "My brothers and my brethren, behold I say unto you, how great reason have we to rejoice; for could we have supposed when we started from the land of Zarahemla that God would have granted unto us such great blessings? And now, I ask, what great blessings has he bestowed upon us? Can ye tell?

"Behold, I answer for you; for our brethren, the Lamanites, were in darkness, yea, even in the darkest abyss, but behold, how many of them are brought to behold the marvelous light of God! And this is the blessing which hath been bestowed upon us, that we have been made instruments in the hands of God to bring about this great work.

"Behold, thousands of them do rejoice, and have been brought into the fold of God. Behold, the field was ripe, and blessed are ye, for ye did thrust in the sickle, and did reap with your might, yea, all the day long did ye labor; and behold the number of your sheaves! And they shall be gathered into the garners, that they are not wasted.

"Yea, they shall not be beaten down by the storm at the last day; yea, neither shall they be harrowed up by the whirlwinds; but when the storm cometh they shall be gathered together in their place, that the storm cannot penetrate to them; yea, neither shall they be driven with fierce winds whithersoever the enemy listeth to carry them. But behold, they are in the hands of the Lord of the harvest, and they are his; and he will raise them up at the last day.

"Blessed be the name of our God; let us sing to his praise, yea, let us give thanks to his holy name, for he doth work righteousness forever. For if we had not come up out of the land of Zarahemla, these our dearly beloved brethren, who have so dearly beloved us, would still have been racked with hatred against us, yea, and they would also have been strangers to God."

Aaron misunderstood his brother's exultation, thinking that he was taking credit to himself. He told Ammon, "I fear that thy joy doth carry thee away unto boasting."

Humble, but joyful, Ammon replied: "I do not boast in my own strength, nor in my own wisdom; but behold, my joy is full, yea, my heart is brim with joy, and I will rejoice in my God."

Still awed but overjoyed by the blessings of the Lord, Ammon reminded his brothers that when they first proposed undertaking this mission to the Lamanites, they were still in a state of repenting from their efforts to destroy the church.

He recalled also that their friends in Zarahemla had criticized them for supposing they could convert any Lamanites.

"For they said unto us: Do ye suppose that ye can bring the Lamanites to the knowledge of the truth? Do ye suppose that ye can convince the Lamanites of the incorrectness of the traditions of their fathers, as stiffnecked a people as they are; whose hearts delight in the shedding of blood; whose days have been spent in the grossest iniquity; whose ways have been the ways of a transgressor from the beginning? Now my brethren, ye remember that this was their language.

"And moreover they did say: Let us take up arms against

them, that we destroy them and their iniquity out of the land, lest they overrun us and destroy us.

"But behold, my beloved brethren, we came into the wilderness not with the intent to destroy our brethren, but with the intent that perhaps we might save some few of their souls. . . .

"Now my brethren, we see that God is mindful of every people, whatsoever land they may be in; yea, he numbereth his people, and his bowels of mercy are over all the earth. Now this is my joy, and my great thanksgiving; yea, and I will give thanks unto my God forever. Amen." (Alma 26.)

Chapter 14

THE MOVE TO JERSHON

The defeated armies of the Lamanites, returning from their attack on the Nephites, mourned the heavy losses that they had suffered. Many of the Amalekites had also been killed, for they had joined the Lamanite army and had, in fact, urged the Lamanites to start this war. The defeat of their army and their own heavy losses encouraged them greatly to hate the Nephites more than ever.

When the Amalekites realized that it was useless to go again against Zarahemla, they again turned their anger upon the defenseless people of Anti-Nephi-Lehi. They made renewed attacks on them and killed many.

The people of Anti-Nephi-Lehi again refused to take their arms, and "they suffered themselves to be slain according to the desires of their enemies.

"Now when Ammon and his brethren saw this work of destruction among those whom they so dearly beloved, and among those who had so dearly beloved them—for they were treated as though they were angels sent from God to save them from everlasting destruction—therefore, when Ammon and his brethren saw this great work of destruction, they were moved with compassion, and they said unto the king: Let us gather together this people of the Lord, and let us go down to the land of Zarahemla to our brethren the Nephites, and flee out of the hands of our enemies, that we be not destroyed."

The king, who was afraid to live among the Nephites because of their cruelty in past wars, said, "Behold, the Nephites will destroy us, because of the many murders and sins we have committed against them."

As a prophet, Ammon knew he must seek revelation from God.

"And Ammon said: I will go and inquire of the Lord, and if he say unto us, go down unto our brethren, will ye go?

"And the king said unto him: Yea, if the Lord saith unto us go, we will go down unto our brethren, and we will be their slaves until we repair unto them the many murders and sins which we have committed against them.

"But Ammon said unto him: It is against the law of our brethren, which was established by my father, that there should be any slaves among them; therefore let us go down and rely upon the mercies of our brethren.

"But the king said unto him: Inquire of the Lord, and if he saith unto us go, we will go; otherwise we will perish in the land."

Ammon went to the Lord, who commanded him: "Get this people out of this land, that they perish not; for Satan has great hold on the hearts of the Amalekites, who do stir up the Lamanites to anger against their brethren to slay them; therefore get thee out of this land; and blessed are this people in this generation, for I will preserve them."

The king now agreed, "and they gathered together all their people, yea, all the people of the Lord, and did gather together all their flocks and herds, and departed out of the land, and came into the wilderness which divided the land of Nephi from the land of Zarahemla, and came over near the borders of the land."

When the people of Anti-Nephi-Lehi neared Zarahemla, Ammon said, "Behold, I and my brethren will go forth into the land of Zarahemla, and ye shall remain here until we return; and we will try the hearts of our brethren, whether they will that ye shall come into their land."

The main body of the people waited in the wilderness while Ammon and his brothers went to the city. As they traveled the highway, to their great surprise they met the prophet Alma on his way back from the land Gideon. (Alma 27:1-16.)

"Now these sons of Mosiah were with Alma at the time the

angel first appeared unto him; therefore Alma did rejoice exceedingly to see his brethren; and what added more to his joy, they were still his brethren in the Lord; yea, and they had waxed strong in the knowledge of the truth; for they were men of a sound understanding and they had searched the scriptures diligently, that they might know the word of God." (Alma 17:2.)

What a joyful meeting! The sons of Mosiah had been preaching the word for fourteen years, and they were overjoyed to see Alma again after so long a time.

"Now the joy of Ammon was so great even that he was full; yea, he was swallowed up in the joy of his God, even to the exhausting of his strength; and he fell again to the earth. Now was not this exceeding joy? Behold, this is joy which none receiveth save it be the truly penitent and humble seeker of happiness. Now the joy of Alma in meeting his brethren was truly great, and also the joy of Aaron, of Omner, and Himni; but behold their joy was not that to exceed their strength."

The sons of Mosiah explained to Alma the purpose of their journey, and "Alma conducted his brethren back to the land of Zarahemla; even to his own house. And they went and told the chief judge all the things that had happened unto them in the land of Nephi, among their brethren, the Lamanites."

The response of the Nephites was all that Ammon could expect.

"The chief judge sent a proclamation throughout all the land, desiring the voice of the people concerning the admitting their brethren, who were the people of Anti-Nephi-Lehi.

"And it came to pass that the voice of the people came, saying: Behold, we will give up the land of Jershon, which is on the east by the sea, which joins the land Bountiful, which is on the south of the land Bountiful; and this land Jershon is the land which we will give unto our brethren for an inheritance.

"And behold, we will set our armies between the land Jershon and the land Nephi, that we may protect our brethren in the land Jershon; and this we do for our brethren, on account of their fear to take up arms against their brethren lest they should commit sin; and this their great fear came because of their sore repentance which they had, on account of their many murders and their awful wickedness.

"And now behold, this will we do unto our brethren, that they may inherit the land Jershon; and we will guard them from their enemies with our armies, on condition that they will give us a portion of their substance to assist us that we may maintain our armies."

Alma now joined Ammon in returning to the wilderness, where the people of Anti-Nephi-Lehi awaited them.

"And it came to pass that it did cause great joy among them. And they went down into the land of Jershon, and took possession of the land of Jershon; and they were called by the Nephites the people of Ammon; therefore they were distinguished by that name ever after.

"And they were among the people of Nephi, and also numbered among the people who were of the church of God. And they were also distinguished for their zeal towards God, and also towards men; for they were perfectly honest and upright in all things; and they were firm in the faith of Christ, even unto the end.

"And they did look upon shedding the blood of their brethren with the greatest abhorrence; and they never could be prevailed upon to take up arms against their brethren; and they never did look upon death with any degree of terror, for their hope and views of Christ and the resurrection; therefore, death was swallowed up to them by the victory of Christ over it.

"Therefore, they would suffer death in the most aggravating and distressing manner which could be inflicted by their brethren, before they would take the sword or cimeter to smite them.

"And thus they were a zealous and beloved people, a highly favored people of the Lord." (Alma 27:17-30.)

Chapter 15

LAMANITE REVENGE

The people of Anti-Nephi-Lehi established themselves in the land of Jershon. The church was organized among them, and they were fully accepted by the Nephites, who stationed an army there to protect them in case of attack. They kept their covenant never to take up arms again.

It was not long until the cry of war came once more. The armies of the Lamanites had followed these travelers to the land of Zarahemla, and they now attacked this city. Severe losses occurred in spite of the protection the Nephite army provided for the people of Anti-Nephi-Lehi.

"And thus there was a tremendous battle; yea, even such an one as never had been known among all the people in the land from the time Lehi left Jerusalem; yea, and tens of thousands of the Lamanites were slain and scattered abroad.

"Yea, and also there was a tremendous slaughter among the people of Nephi; nevertheless, the Lamanites were driven and scattered, and the people of Nephi returned again to their land.

"And now this was a time that there was a great mourning and lamentation heard throughout all the land, among all the people of Nephi—yea, the cry of widows mourning for their husbands, and also of fathers mourning for their sons, and the daughter for the brother, yea, the brother for the father; and thus the cry of mourning was heard among all of them, mourning for their kindred who had been slain.

"And now surely this was a sorrowful day; yea, a time of solemnity, and a time of much fasting and prayer." (Alma 28: 1-6.)

Later when the Lamanites came again in an effort to destroy

the Nephites, the people of Anti-Nephi-Lehi wished to aid the Nephite defense in some way. They furnished much food and other supplies to the Nephites.

"Because of their oath they had been kept from taking up arms against their brethren; for they had taken an oath that they never would shed blood more; and according to their oath they would have perished; yea, they would have suffered themselves to have fallen into the hands of their brethren, had it not been for the pity and the exceeding love which Ammon and his brethren had had for them.

"And for this cause they were brought down into the land of Zarahemla; and they ever had been protected by the Nephites.

"But it came to pass that when they saw the danger, and the many afflictions and tribulations which the Nephites bore for them, they were moved with compassion and were desirous to take up arms in the defence of their country. But behold, as they were about to take their weapons of war, they were over-powered by the persuasions of Helaman and his brethren, for they were about to break the oath which they had made.

"And Helaman feared lest by so doing they should lose their souls; therefore all those who had entered into this covenant were compelled to behold their brethren wade through their af-flictions, in their dangerous circumstances at this time."

But this people had many sons who had never taken the oath. The sons could help defend their country. They could take up arms.

Thus, two thousand young sons of the people of Ammon now joined the Nephite army under the command of a man named Helaman.

"And they were all young men, and they were exceedingly valiant for courage, and also for strength and activity; but be-hold, this was not all—they were men who were true at all times in whatsoever thing they were entrusted. Yea, they were men of truth and soberness, for they had been taught to keep the com-mandments of God and to walk uprightly before him.

"And now it came to pass that Helaman did march at the

head of his two thousand stripling soldiers, to the support of the people in the borders of the land on the south by the west sea." (Alma 53:11-22.)

Helaman later wrote to Moroni, the Nephite commander, concerning them: "I, Helaman, did march at the head of these two thousand young men to the city of Judea, to assist Antipus, whom ye had appointed a leader over the people of that part of the land. And I did join my two thousand sons, (for they are worthy to be called sons) to the army of Antipus, in which strength Antipus did rejoice exceedingly; for behold, his army had been reduced by the Lamanites because their forces had slain a vast number of our men, for which cause we have to mourn." (Alma 56:9-10.)

Helaman further wrote of a severe battle in which these young men took part. Viciously attacked by the Lamanites, the Nephites retreated.

"And now Antipus, beholding our danger, did speed the march of his army. But behold, it was night; therefore they did not overtake us, neither did Antipus overtake them; therefore we did camp for the night.

"And it came to pass that before the dawn of the morning, behold, the Lamanites were pursuing us. Now we were not sufficiently strong to contend with them; yea, I would not suffer that my little sons should fall into their hands; therefore we did continue our march, and we took our march into the wilderness.

"Now they durst not turn to the right nor to the left lest they should be surrounded; neither would I turn to the right nor to the left lest they should overtake me, and we could not stand against them, but be slain, and they would make their escape; and thus we did flee all that day into the wilderness, even until it was dark. And it came to pass that again, when the light of the morning came we saw the Lamanites upon us, and we did flee before them."

Helaman continued his letter to the great commander, Moroni, with these words: "And now, whether they were overtaken by Antipus we knew not, but I said unto my men: Behold, we know not but they have halted for the purpose that we should come against them, that they might catch us in their snare; therefore what say ye, my sons, will ye go against them to battle?

"And now I say unto you, my beloved brother Moroni, that never had I seen so great courage, nay, not amongst all the Nephites. For as I had ever called them my sons (for they were all of them very young) even so they said unto me: Father, behold our God is with us, and he will not suffer that we should fall; then let us go forth; we would not slay our brethren if they would let us alone; therefore let us go, lest they should overpower the army of Antipus.

"Now they never had fought, yet they did not fear death; and they did think more upon the liberty of their fathers than they did upon their lives; yea, they had been taught by their mothers, that if they did not doubt, God would deliver them. And they rehearsed unto me the words of their mothers, saying: We do not doubt our mothers knew it."

Helaman now ordered his two thousand stripling soldiers to attack the Lamanites from the rear. They had trapped the Nephite commander, Antipus, and his weary men.

"The army of Antipus being weary, because of their long march in so short a space of time, were about to fall into the hands of the Lamanites; and had I not returned with my two thousand they would have obtained their purpose. For Antipus had fallen by the sword, and many of his leaders, because of their weariness, which was occasioned by the speed of their march—therefore the men of Antipus, being confused because of the fall of their leaders, began to give way before the Lamanites.

"And it came to pass that the Lamanites took courage, and began to pursue them; and thus were the Lamanites pursuing them with great vigor when Helaman came upon their rear with his two thousand, and began to slay them exceedingly, insomuch that the whole army of the Lamanites halted and turned upon Helaman.

"Now when the people of Antipus saw that the Lamanites had turned them about, they gathered together their men and came again upon the rear of the Lamanites.

"And now it came to pass that we, the people of Nephi, the people of Antipus, and I with my two thousand, did surround the Lamanites, and did slay them; yea, insomuch that they were compelled to deliver up their weapons of war and also themselves as prisoners of war.

"And now it came to pass that when they had surrendered themselves up unto us, behold, I numbered those young men who had fought with me, fearing lest there were many of them slain.

"But behold, to my great joy, there had not one soul of them fallen to the earth; yea, and they had fought as if with the strength of God; yea, never were men known to have fought with such miraculous strength; and with such mighty power did they fall upon the Lamanites, that they did frighten them; and for this cause did the Lamanites deliver themselves up as prisoners of war." (Alma 56:38-56.)

Helaman described still another encounter in which his two thousand stripling soldiers fought. He said:

"But behold, my little band of two thousand and sixty fought most desperately; yea, they were firm before the Lamanites, and did administer death unto all those who opposed them.

"And as the remainder of our army were about to give way before the Lamanites, behold, those two thousand and sixty were firm and undaunted. Yea, and they did obey and observe to perform every word of command with exactness; yea, and even according to their faith it was done unto them; and I did remember the words which they said unto me that their mothers had taught them. . . .

"And it came to pass that there were two hundred, out of my two thousand and sixty, who had fainted because of the loss of blood; nevertheless, according to the goodness of God, and to our great astonishment, and also the joy of our whole army, there was not one soul of them who did perish; yea, and neither was there one soul among them who had not received many wounds.

"And now, their preservation was astonishing to our whole army, yea, that they should be spared while there was a thousand of our brethren who were slain. And we do justly ascribe it to the miraculous power of God, because of their exceeding faith in that which they had been taught to believe—that there was a just God, and whosoever did not doubt, that they should be preserved by his marvelous power.

"Now this was the faith of these of whom I have spoken; they are young, and their minds are firm, and they do put their trust in God continually." (Alma 57:19-21, 25-27.)

The people of Ammon, formerly called the Anti-Nephi-Lehies, now became fully absorbed into the Nephite nation, though they still preserved their oath of peace. They continued to build up their communities, obeyed the gospel, and supported the Nephite cause, thus providing a constant example of the way in which true followers of Christ should live.

The work of Mosiah's sons had brought a truly bounteous harvest for the Lord.

Chapter 16

ANOTHER LAMANITE MISSION

About thirty years before the birth of the Savior, a great states-
man named Nephi was chief judge among the Nephites. He was
a grandson of Helaman, who had led the two thousand young
soldiers into war, and his father was also named Helaman.

In the days of Nephi there was great wickedness among the
Nephites, who had many encounters with the Lamanites and
often were defeated. Because of their sinful lives, the Lord no
longer prospered their efforts, and they feared any further wars.

"And it came to pass, because of the greatness of the
number of the Lamanites the Nephites were in great fear, lest
they should be overpowered, and trodden down, and slain, and
destroyed. . . .

"And because of their iniquity the church had begun to
dwindle; and they began to disbelieve in the spirit of prophecy
and in the spirit of revelation; and the judgments of God did
stare them in the face.

"And they saw that they had become weak, like unto their
brethren, the Lamanites, and that the Spirit of the Lord did no
more preserve them; yea, it had withdrawn from them because
the Spirit of the Lord doth not dwell in unholy temples—therefore the Lord did cease to preserve them by his miraculous and
matchless power, for they had fallen into a state of unbelief and
awful wickedness; and they saw that the Lamanites were exceedingly more numerous than they, and except they should
cleave unto the Lord their God they must unavoidably perish."
(Helaman 4:20, 23-25.)

In this critical time Nephi gave up the judgment seat "and
took it upon him to preach the word of God all the remainder of

his days, and his brother Lehi also, all the remainder of his days; for they remembered the words which their father Helaman spake unto them. And these are the words which he spake:

"Behold, my sons, I desire that ye should remember to keep the commandments of God; and I would that ye should declare unto the people these words. Behold, I have given unto you the names of our first parents who came out of the land of Jerusalem; and this I have done that when you remember your names ye may remember them; and when ye remember them ye may remember their works; and when ye remember their works ye may know how that it is said, and also written, that they were good."

Nephi and Lehi went from city to city among the Nephites crying repentance and then turned to the Lamanites.

"And it came to pass that Nephi and Lehi did preach unto the Lamanites with such great power and authority; for they had power and authority given unto them that they might speak, and they also had what they should speak given unto them—therefore they did speak unto the great astonishment of the Lamanites, to the convincing them, insomuch that there were eight thousand of the Lamanites who were in the land of Zarahemla and round about baptized unto repentance, and were convinced of the wickedness of the traditions of their fathers."

They went to the land of Nephi, the area where Ammon and his brothers had labored.

"And it came to pass that they were taken by an army of the Lamanites and cast into prison; yea, even in that same prison in which Ammon and his brethren were cast by the servants of Limhi.

"And after they had been cast into prison many days without food, behold, they went forth into the prison to take them that they might slay them.

"And it came to pass that Nephi and Lehi were encircled about as if by fire, even insomuch that they durst not lay their hands upon them for fear lest they should be burned. Nevertheless, Nephi and Lehi were not burned; and they were as standing in the midst of fire and were not burned. And when they saw that they were encircled about with a pillar of fire, and that it burned them not, their hearts did take courage. For they saw that the Lamanites durst not lay their hands upon them; neither durst they come near unto them, but stood as if they were struck dumb with amazement."

Nephi and Lehi now began to speak to them, saying, "Fear not, for behold, it is God that has shown unto you this marvelous thing, in the which is shown unto you that ye cannot lay your hands on us to slay us."

An earthquake shook the prison, but the walls did not fall.

"And it came to pass that they were overshadowed with a cloud of darkness, and an awful solemn fear came upon them. And it came to pass that there came a voice as if it were above the cloud of darkness, saying: Repent ye, repent ye, and seek no more to destroy my servants whom I have sent unto you to declare good tidings.

"And it came to pass when they heard this voice, and beheld that it was not a voice of thunder, neither was it a voice of a great tumultuous noise, but behold, it was a still voice of perfect mildness, as if it had been a whisper, and it did pierce even to the very soul."

The earth trembled again. "The voice came again, saying: Repent ye, repent ye, for the kingdom of heaven is at hand; and seek no more to destroy my servants. And it came to pass that the earth shook again, and the walls trembled.

"And also again the third time the voice came, and did speak unto them marvelous words which cannot be uttered by man; and the walls did tremble again, and the earth shook as if it were about to divide asunder."

Frightened as they were, the Lamanites could not run away because of the dense cloud that covered them.

"Now there was one among them who was a Nephite by birth, who had once belonged to the church of God but had dissented from them. And it came to pass that he turned him about, and behold, he saw through the cloud of darkness the faces of

Nephi and Lehi; and behold, they did shine exceedingly, even as the faces of angels. And he beheld that they did lift their eyes to heaven; and they were in the attitude as if talking or lifting their voices to some being whom they beheld."

This man called to everyone to look toward Nephi and Lehi, and "there was power given unto them that they did turn and look; and they did behold the faces of Nephi and Lehi.

"And they said unto the man: Behold, what do all these things mean, and who is it with whom these men do converse?

"Now the man's name was Aminadab. And Aminadab said unto them: They do converse with the angels of God.

"And it came to pass that the Lamanites said unto him: What shall we do, that this cloud of darkness may be removed from overshadowing us?

"And Aminadab said unto them: You must repent, and cry unto the voice, even until ye shall have faith in Christ."

Finally the cloud began to lift, and "they saw that they were encircled about, yea every soul, by a pillar of fire. And Nephi and Lehi were in the midst of them; yea, they were encircled about; yea, they were as if in the midst of a flaming fire, yet it did harm them not, neither did it take hold upon the walls of the prison; and they were filled with that joy which is unspeakable and full of glory.

"And behold, the Holy Spirit of God did come down from heaven, and did enter into their hearts, and they were filled as if with fire, and they could speak forth marvelous words.

"And it came to pass that there came a voice unto them, yea, a pleasant voice, as if it were a whisper, saying: Peace, peace be unto you, because of your faith in my Well Beloved, who was from the foundation of the world. . . .

"When they heard this they cast up their eyes as if to behold from whence the voice came; and behold, they saw the heavens open; and angels came down out of heaven and ministered unto them."

Some three hundred persons witnessed this miracle.

"And it came to pass that they did go forth, and did minister unto the people, declaring throughout all the regions round about all the things which they had heard and seen, insomuch that the more part of the Lamanites were convinced of them, because of the greatness of the evidences which they had received.

"And as many as were convinced did lay down their weapons of war, and also their hatred and the tradition of their fathers. And it came to pass that they did yield up unto the Nephites the lands of their possession." (Helaman 5.)

Chapter 17

THE LAMANITES PREACH

Conversions continued to increase among the Lamanites, who became more righteous than the Nephites.

"For behold, there were many of the Nephites who had become hardened and impenitent and grossly wicked, insomuch that they did reject the word of God and all the preaching and prophesying which did come among them.

"Nevertheless, the people of the church did have great joy because of the conversion of the Lamanites, yea, because of the church of God, which had been established among them. And they did fellowship one with another, and did rejoice one with another, and did have great joy."

They came into the city of Zarahemla and told the people of the manner of their own conversion "and did exhort them to faith and repentance. Yea, and many did preach with exceedingly great power and authority, unto the bringing down many of them into the depths of humility, to be the humble followers of God and the Lamb."

Peace came to the whole land. Enmities disappeared, and the "Nephites did go into whatsoever part of the land they would, whether among the Nephites or the Lamanites. And it came to pass that the Lamanites did also go whithersoever they would, whether it were among the Lamanites or among the Nephites; and thus they did have free intercourse one with another, to buy and to sell, and to get gain, according to their desire."

The people now became "rich, both the Lamanites and the Nephites; and they did have an exceeding plenty of gold, and of silver, and of all manner of precious metals, both in the land south and in the land north.

"Now the land south was called Lehi, and the land north was called Mulek, which was after the son of Zedekiah; for the Lord did bring Mulek into the land north, and Lehi into the land south.

"And behold, there was all manner of gold in both these lands, and of silver, and of precious ore of every kind; and there were also curious workmen, who did work all kinds of ore and did refine it; and thus they did become rich.

"They did raise grain in abundance, both in the north and in the south; and they did flourish exceedingly, both in the north and in the south. And they did multiply and wax exceedingly strong in the land. And they did raise many flocks and herds, yea, many fatlings.

"Behold their women did toil and spin, and did make all manner of cloth, of fine-twined linen and cloth of every kind, to clothe their nakedness."

But crime raised its head again. When Nephi gave up the judgment seat, Cezoram succeeded him. Now, breaking this era of peace and prosperity, "Cezoram was murdered by an unknown hand as he sat upon the judgment-seat. And it came to pass that in the same year, that his son, who had been appointed by the people in his stead, was also murdered. . . .

"The Lord had blessed them so long with the riches of the world that they had not been stirred up to anger, to wars, nor to bloodshed; therefore they began to set their hearts upon their riches; yea, they began to seek to get gain that they might be lifted up one above another; therefore they began to commit secret murders, and to rob and to plunder, that they might get gain.

"And now behold, those murderers and plunderers were a band who had been formed by Kishkumen and Gadianton. And now it had come to pass that there were many, even among the Nephites, of Gadianton's band. But behold, they were more numerous among the more wicked part of the Lamanites. And they were called Gadianton's robbers and murderers.

"And it was they who did murder the chief judge Cezoram, and his son, while in the judgment-seat; and behold, they were not found.

"And now it came to pass that when the Lamanites found that there were robbers among them they were exceedingly sorrowful; and they did use every means in their power to destroy them off the face of the earth."

Here again the converted Lamanites became the shining lights for the day:

"And thus we see that the Nephites did begin to dwindle in unbelief, and grow in wickedness and abominations, while the Lamanites began to grow exceedingly in the knowledge of their God; yea, they did begin to keep his statutes and commandments, and to walk in truth and uprightness before him.

"And thus we see that the Spirit of the Lord began to withdraw from the Nephites, because of the wickedness and the hardness of their hearts.

"And thus we see that the Lord began to pour out his Spirit upon the Lamanites, because of their easiness and willingness to believe in his words.

"And it came to pass that the Lamanites did hunt the band of robbers of Gadianton; and they did preach the word of God among the more wicked part of them, insomuch that this band of robbers was utterly destroyed from among the Lamanites." (Helaman 6:1-20, 34-37.)

Chapter 18

SAMUEL
THE LAMANITE

With the increasing wickedness of the Nephites and the growing spirituality of the Lamanites, the Lord raised up another prophet in the land, and he was a Lamanite.

Samuel, the Lord's new servant, came to the chief Nephite city, Zarahemla, and there "began to preach unto the people. And it came to pass that he did preach, many days, repentance unto the people, and they did cast him out, and he was about to return to his own land."

But the Lord wanted a further warning to be given. He sent Samuel back to the city, but the people would not let him through the gates. That did not deter him; he climbed on the wall surrounding the city and preached from there, saying:

"Behold, I, Samuel, a Lamanite, do speak the words of the Lord which he doth put into my heart; and behold he hath put it into my heart to say unto this people that the sword of justice hangeth over this people; and four hundred years pass not away save the sword of justice falleth upon this people.

"Yea, heavy destruction awaiteth this people, and it surely cometh unto this people, and nothing can save this people save it be repentance and faith on the Lord Jesus Christ, who surely shall come into the world, and shall suffer many things and shall be slain for his people."

Speaking for the Lord, Samuel threatened Zarahemla with destruction if the people failed to repent.

"Yea, wo unto this great city of Zarahemla; for behold, it is because of those who are righteous that it is saved; yea, wo unto this great city, for I perceive, saith the Lord, that there are many, yea, even the more part of this great city, that will harden their hearts against me, saith the Lord.

"But blessed are they who will repent, for them will I spare. But behold, if it were not for the righteous who are in this great city, behold, I would cause that fire should come down out of heaven and destroy it.

"But behold, it is for the righteous' sake that it is spared. But behold, the time cometh, saith the Lord, that when ye shall cast out the righteous from among you, then shall ye be ripe for destruction; yea, wo be unto this great city, because of the wickedness and abominations which are in her."

Then he continued:

"Behold, a curse shall come upon the land, saith the Lord of Hosts, because of the peoples' sake who are upon the land, yea, because of their wickedness and their abominations.

"And it shall come to pass, saith the Lord of Hosts, yea, our great and true God, that whoso shall hide up treasures in the earth shall find them again no more, because of the great curse of the land, save he be a righteous man and shall hide it up unto the Lord.

"For I will, saith the Lord, that they shall hide up their treasures unto me; and cursed be they who hide not up their treasures unto me; for none hideth up their treasures unto me save it be the righteous; and he that hideth not up his treasures unto me, cursed is he, and also the treasure, and none shall redeem it because of the curse of the land.

"And the day shall come that they shall hide up their treasures, because they have set their hearts upon riches; and because they have set their hearts upon their riches, and will hide up their treasures when they shall flee before their enemies; because they will not hide them up unto me, cursed be they and also their treasures; and in that day shall they be smitten, saith the Lord."

Samuel gave this warning:

"Therefore, thus saith the Lord: Because of the hardness of

the hearts of the people of the Nephites, except they repent I will take away my word from them, and I will withdraw my Spirit from them, and I will suffer them no longer, and I will turn the hearts of their brethren against them.

"And four hundred years shall not pass away before I will cause that they shall be smitten; yea, I will visit them with the sword and with famine and with pestilence.

"Yea, I will visit them in my fierce anger, and there shall be those of the fourth generation who shall live, of your enemies, to behold your utter destruction; and this shall surely come except ye repent, saith the Lord; and those of the fourth generation shall visit your destruction.

"But if ye will repent and return unto the Lord your God I will turn away mine anger, saith the Lord; yea, thus saith the Lord, blessed are they who will repent and turn unto me, but wo unto him that repenteth not." (Helaman 13:1-20.)

Then he spoke of the coming of Christ.

"Behold, I give unto you a sign; for five years more cometh, and behold, then cometh the Son of God to redeem all those who shall believe on his name.

"And behold, this will I give unto you for a sign at the time of his coming; for behold, there shall be great lights in heaven, insomuch that in the night before he cometh there shall be no darkness, insomuch that it shall appear unto man as if it was day.

"Therefore, there shall be one day and a night and a day, as if it were one day and there were no night; and this shall be unto you for a sign; for ye shall know of the rising of the sun and also of its setting; therefore they shall know of a surety that there shall be two days and a night; nevertheless the night shall not be darkened; and it shall be the night before he is born.

"And behold, there shall a new star arise, such an one as ye never have beheld; and this also shall be a sign unto you.

"And behold this is not all, there shall be many signs and wonders in heaven. And it shall come to pass that ye shall all be amazed, and wonder, insomuch that ye shall fall to the earth.

"And it shall come to pass that whosoever shall believe on the Son of God, the same shall have everlasting life."

He told them that he had been visited by an angel, who commanded him to announce these prophecies.

"And now, because I am a Lamanite, and have spoken unto you the words which the Lord hath commanded me, and because it was hard against you, ye are angry with me and do seek to destroy me, and have cast me out from among you.

"And ye shall hear my words, for, for this intent have I come up upon the walls of this city, that ye might hear and know of the judgments of God which do await you because of your iniquities, and also that ye might know the conditions of repentance; and also that ye might know of the coming of Jesus Christ, the Son of God, the Father of heaven and of earth, the Creator of all things from the beginning; and that ye might know of the signs of his coming, to the intent that ye might believe on his name.

"And if ye believe on his name ye will repent of all your sins, that thereby ye may have a remission of them through his merits."

But Samuel had still another important prophecy. It had to do with conditions in America at the death of Christ.

"And behold, again, another sign I give unto you, yea, a sign of his death. For behold, he surely must die that salvation may come; yea, it behooveth him and becometh expedient that he dieth, to bring to pass the resurrection of the dead, that thereby men may be brought into the presence of the Lord. . . .

"But behold, as I said unto you concerning another sign, a sign of his death, behold, in that day that he shall suffer death the sun shall be darkened and refuse to give his light unto you; and also the moon and the stars; and there shall be no light upon the face of this land, even from the time that he shall suffer death, for the space of three days, to the time that he shall rise again from the dead.

"Yea, at the time that he shall yield up the ghost there shall be thunderings and lightnings for the space of many hours, and the earth shall shake and tremble; and the rocks which are upon the face of this earth, which are both above the earth and beneath, which ye know at this time are solid, or the more part of it is one solid mass, shall be broken up; yea, they shall be rent in twain, and shall ever after be found in seams and in cracks, and in broken fragments upon the face of the whole earth, yea, both above the earth and beneath.

"And behold, there shall be great tempests, and there shall be many mountains laid low, like unto a valley, and there shall be many places which are now called valleys which shall become mountains, whose height is great. And many highways shall be broken up, and many cities shall become desolate. And many graves shall be opened, and shall yield up many of their dead; and many saints shall appear unto many.

"And behold, thus hath the angel spoken unto me; for he said unto me that there should be thunderings and lightnings for the space of many hours. And he said unto me that while the thunder and the lightning lasted, and the tempest, that these things should be, and that darkness should cover the face of the whole earth for the space of three days."

Samuel stressed to the people the fact that they had their own free agency and would be held fully accountable for their own acts, but he strongly urged them to repent.

"And now remember, remember, my brethren, that whosoever perisheth, perisheth unto himself; and whosoever doeth iniquity, doeth it unto himself; for behold, ye are free; ye are permitted to act for yourselves; for behold, God hath given unto you a knowledge and he hath made you free." (Helaman 14.)

Many who heard Samuel believed what he said and went to Nephi to receive baptism.

"But as many as there were who did not believe in the words of Samuel were angry with him; and they cast stones at him upon the wall, and also many shot arrows at him as he stood upon the wall; but the Spirit of the Lord was with him, insomuch that they could not hit him with their stones neither with their arrows.

"Now when they saw that they could not hit him, there were many more who did believe on his words, insomuch that they went away unto Nephi to be baptized. . . .

"But the more part of them did not believe in the words of Samuel; therefore when they saw that they could not hit him with their stones and their arrows, they cried unto their captains, saying: Take this fellow and bind him, for behold he hath a devil; and because of the power of the devil which is in him we cannot hit him with our stones and our arrows; therefore take him and bind him, and away with him.

"And as they went forth to lay their hands on him, behold, he did cast himself down from the wall, and did flee out of their lands, yea, even unto his own country, and began to preach and to prophesy among his own people.

"And behold, he was never heard of more among the Nephites; and thus were the affairs of the people." (Helaman 16:1-8.)

Chapter 19

ALL CONVERTS UNITE

In the period just before the birth of Christ, the Gadianton robbers became very numerous. They constantly attacked both Lamanites and Nephites.

"And it came to pass in the thirteenth year there began to be wars and contentions throughout all the land; for the Gadianton robbers had become so numerous, and did slay so many of the people, and did lay waste so many cities, and did spread so much death and carnage throughout the land, that it became expedient that all the people, both the Nephites and the Lamanites, should take up arms against them.

"Therefore, all the Lamanites who had become converted unto the Lord did unite with their brethren, the Nephites, and were compelled, for the safety of their lives and their women and their children, to take up arms against those Gadianton robbers, yea, and also to maintain their rights, and the privileges of their church and of their worship, and their freedom and their liberty. . . .

"And it came to pass that those Lamanites who had united with the Nephites were numbered among the Nephites; and their curse was taken from them, and their skin became white like unto the Nephites; and their young men and their daughters became exceedingly fair, and they were numbered among the Nephites, and were called Nephites. And thus ended the thirteenth year." (3 Nephi 2:11-16.)

Following the universal conversion of Lamanites and Nephites after the Savior's visitation in America, Lamanites and Nephites ceased to live as separate peoples. All became one nation.

The chosen disciples of Jesus formed branches of the church "in all the lands round about. . . .

"And it came to pass in the thirty and sixth year, the people were all converted unto the Lord, upon all the face of the land, both Nephites and Lamanites, and there were no contentions and disputations among them, and every man did deal justly one with another.

"And they had all things common among them; therefore there were not rich and poor, bond and free, but they were all made free, and partakers of the heavenly gift.

"And it came to pass that the thirty and seventh year passed away also, and there still continued to be peace in the land.

"And there were great and marvelous works wrought by the disciples of Jesus, insomuch that they did heal the sick, and raise the dead, and cause the lame to walk, and the blind to receive their sight, and the deaf to hear; and all manner of miracles did they work among the children of men; and in nothing did they work miracles save it were in the name of Jesus."

The population steadily grew "and became an exceedingly fair and delightsome people. . . .

"And it came to pass that there was no contention in the land, because of the love of God which did dwell in the hearts of the people.

"And there were no envyings, nor strifes, nor tumults, nor whoredoms, nor lyings, nor murders, nor any manner of lasciviousness; and surely there could not be a happier people among all the people who had been created by the hand of God.

"There were no robbers, nor murderers, neither were there Lamanites, nor any manner of -ites: but they were in one, the children of Christ, and heirs to the kingdom of God."

But after two hundred years of peace, things began to change. The people "were lifted up in pride, such as the wearing of costly apparel, and all manner of fine pearls, and of the fine things of the world. And from that time forth they did have their goods and their substance no more common among them. And they began to be divided into classes; and they began to build up churches unto themselves to get gain, and began to deny the true church of Christ."

They turned against the three Nephite disciples "and they did cast them into prison; but by the power of the word of God, which was in them, the prisons were rent in twain, and they went forth doing mighty miracles among them.

"Nevertheless, and notwithstanding all these miracles, the people did harden their hearts, and did seek to kill them, even as the Jews at Jerusalem sought to kill Jesus, according to his word. And they did cast them into furnaces of fire, and they came forth receiving no harm. And they also cast them into dens of wild beasts, and they did play with the wild beasts even as a child with a lamb; and they did come forth from among them, receiving no harm."

In the 231st year after the coming of Christ, the people again divided into separate factions.

"And it came to pass that they who rejected the gospel were called Lamanites, and Lemuelites, and Ishmaelites; and they did not dwindle in unbelief, but they did wilfully rebel against the gospel of Christ; and they did teach their children that they should not believe, even as their fathers, from the beginning, did dwindle.

"And it was because of the wickedness and abomination of their fathers, even as it was in the beginning. And they were taught to hate the children of God, even as the Lamanites were taught to hate the children of Nephi from the beginning." (4 Nephi.)

The false traditions of the original Lamanites were revived and hatred increased. These old traditions were described fully in the days of Mosiah:

"Now, the Lamanites knew nothing concerning the Lord, nor the strength of the Lord, therefore they depended upon their own strength. Yet they were a strong people, as to the strength of men.

"They were a wild, and ferocious, and a blood-thirsty people, believing in the tradition of their fathers, which is this—Believing that they were driven out of the land of Jerusalem because of the iniquities of their fathers, and that they were wronged in the wilderness by their brethren, and they were also wronged while crossing the sea; and again, that they were wronged while in the land of their first inheritance, after they had crossed the sea, and all this because that Nephi was more faithful in keeping the commandments of the Lord—therefore he was favored of the Lord, for the Lord heard his prayers and answered them, and he took the lead of their journey in the wilderness.

"And his brethren were wroth with him because they understood not the dealings of the Lord; they were also wroth with him upon the waters because they hardened their hearts against the Lord.

"And again, they were wroth with him when they had arrived in the promised land, because they said that he had taken the ruling of the people out of their hands; and they sought to kill him.

"And again, they were wroth with him because he departed into the wilderness as the Lord had commanded him, and took the records which were engraven on the plates of brass, for they said that he robbed them.

"And thus they have taught their children that they should hate them, and that they should murder them, and that they should rob and plunder them, and do all they could to destroy them; therefore they have an eternal hatred towards the children of Nephi." (Mosiah 10:11-17.)

These were the false notions the missionaries to the Lamanites had to counteract. They had been imbedded in each rising generation from the time of Laman and Lemuel. Only the power of God could change them.

Chapter 20

FUTURE PROMISES

From Lehi to Moroni, the early American prophets constantly prayed that the Lord would allow the Lamanites to learn the truth about themselves and their ancestors.

For example, Enos prayed: "I had faith, and I did cry unto God that he would preserve the records; and he covenanted with me that he would bring them forth unto the Lamanites in his own due time." (Enos 1:16.)

And nearly a thousand years later Mormon wrote: "And my prayer to God is concerning my brethren, that they may once again come to the knowledge of God, yea, the redemption of Christ; that they may once again be a delightsome people." (Words of Mormon 1:8.)

The Lord had every intention of answering their prayers, for the Book of Mormon was destined to go to them.

Nephi had written:

"And now, I would prophesy somewhat more concerning the Jews and the Gentiles. For after the book of which I have spoken shall come forth, and be written unto the Gentiles, and sealed up again unto the Lord, there shall be many which shall believe the words which are written; and they shall carry them forth unto the remnant of our seed.

"And then shall the remnant of our seed know concerning us, how that we came out from Jerusalem, and that they are descendants of the Jews.

"And the gospel of Jesus Christ shall be declared among them; wherefore, they shall be restored unto the knowledge of their fathers, and also to the knowledge of Jesus Christ, which was had among their fathers.

"And then shall they rejoice; for they shall know that it is a blessing unto them from the hand of God; and their scales of darkness shall begin to fall from their eyes; and many generations shall not pass away among them, save they shall be a pure and a delightsome people." (2 Nephi 30:3-6.)

The Prophet Joseph Smith prayed for the conversion of the Lamanites. (D&C 109:62-67.) In 1828 the Lord told him:

"And this testimony shall come to the knowledge of the Lamanites, and the Lemuelites, and the Ishmaelites, who dwindled in unbelief because of the iniquity of their fathers, whom the Lord has suffered to destroy their brethren the Nephites, because of their iniquities and their abominations.

"And for this very purpose are these plates preserved, which contain these records—that the promises of the Lord might be fulfilled, which he made to his people; and that the Lamanites might come to the knowledge of their fathers, and that they might know the promises of the Lord, and that they may believe the gospel and rely upon the merits of Jesus Christ, and be glorified through faith in his name, and that through their repentance they might be saved." (D&C 3:18-20.)

And what will be the final result? The Lamanites shall blossom as the rose!

Said the Lord: "But before the great day of the Lord shall come, Jacob shall flourish in the wilderness, and the Lamanites shall blossom as the rose.

"Zion shall flourish upon the hills and rejoice upon the mountains, and shall be assembled together unto the place which I have appointed." (D&C 49:24-25.)

INDEX

to, 9, 15-16; iniquitous state of, 19;
conversion of, through Lamoni's
experiences, 30; king of (Lamoni's
father), 31-33, 38-41; many conversions
among, 41-42; unbelieving, wage war,
44-46; conversion of, after slaying
brethren, 46; Nephites defeat, in battle,
56; Lehi and Nephi preach among, 63;
converted, yield lands to Nephites, 66;
prosperity of, through righteousness,
67-68; destroy Gadianton robbers, 69;
converted, unite with Nephites, 76;
willful rebellion of, 78; hatred of, for
Nephi, 79; promises of the Lord
concerning, 80-81; blossoming of, as
rose, 81
Lamoni, King: Ammon is brought before,
21; accepts Ammon as servant, 21;
mistakes Ammon for the Great Spirit,
23-24; Ammon preaches the gospel to,
25-26; is overpowered by the Spirit, 27;
household of, falls to earth, 28; arises
and bears testimony, 30; father of,
31-33, 38-41; accompanies Ammon to
Middoni, 31-32, 34
Law of Moses, 49
Lehi, land of, 68
Lehi, son of Helaman, 63-65
Liberty, land of, 12-13
Limhi, people of, 16

Middoni, land of, 31, 34, 42
Mormon, 80
Moroni, Helaman's letter to, 58-61
Moses, law of, 49
Mosiah, King: forbids persecution of
church, 3; reign of, 9; successor to,
9-10; proposes system of judges, 10-14;
the people's love for, 13; prays
concerning his sons' mission, 16;
translates the Jaredite record, 16-17;
entrusts records to Alma, 17
Mosiah, sons of. *See* Sons of Mosiah
Mulek, land of, 68

Nehor, 35
Nephi, land of, 15, 38, 63
Nephi, son of Helaman: resigns judgment
seat in order to preach, 62-63;
imprisonment of, 63; is encircled by fire,
63-65
Nephi, son of Lehi, 79-81
Nephites: Lamanites attack cities of, 48;
Lamanite king fears, because of past
wrongs, 52; offer protection to Anti-

Nephi-Lehies, 55; slaughter of, by
Lamanites, 57; iniquity of, made them
weak, 62; Nephi preaches to, 63;
increasing wickedness for, 67, 69;
Samuel the Lamanite preaches to, 70-74;
anger of, at Samuel's words, 74-75;
righteous Lamanites unite with, 76
Noah, King, 11, 36

Peace: covenant of, 44-46, 48, 55;
accompanying conversion, 67-68
Persecution: of church, 3; of the sons of
Mosiah, 34; of Nephi and Lehi, 63; of
the Three Nephites, 78
Pride, 77
Prosperity through righteousness, 67-68, 77

Queen (Lamoni's wife), 27-30
Queen of Lamanites, 39-41

Rebellion: of Alma and the sons of Mosiah,
1; against the church, 2; of apostate
groups, 35-36, 44, 46-47; against the
judges, 68-69
Records, 16-17
Repentance: and forgiveness, 2-3; angel
commands, of Alma, 4; of Alma and the
sons of Mosiah, 7-8; Mosiah's sons
seek, of the Lamanites, 19; of many
Lamanites, 42; heavenly voice
commands, 64; Samuel the Lamanite
preaches, 70-72

Samuel the Lamanite: warns of destruction
of the wicked, 70-72; describes sign of
Christ's birth, 72; prophesies of Christ's
death, 73-74; escapes from angry
listeners, 74-75
Smith, Joseph, 81
Sons of Mosiah: rebellion of, 1-3; names of,
7, 15; repentance of, 7-8; choose
missionary work over kingship, 9-10;
plead to serve Lamanite mission, 15-16;
pray for the Spirit to convert brethren,
18-19; separate to serve missions, 19;
lives of, to be spared, 20; imprisonment
of, 31, 34; decree grants freedom to, for
preaching, 41; missionary successes of,
41-43; reunion of, with Alma, 53-54.
See also Aaron; Ammon
Stripling warriors, two thousand, 57;
courage of, 59; faith of, in their mothers'
teachings, 59; victory of, 59-60;
miraculous deliverance of, 60-61